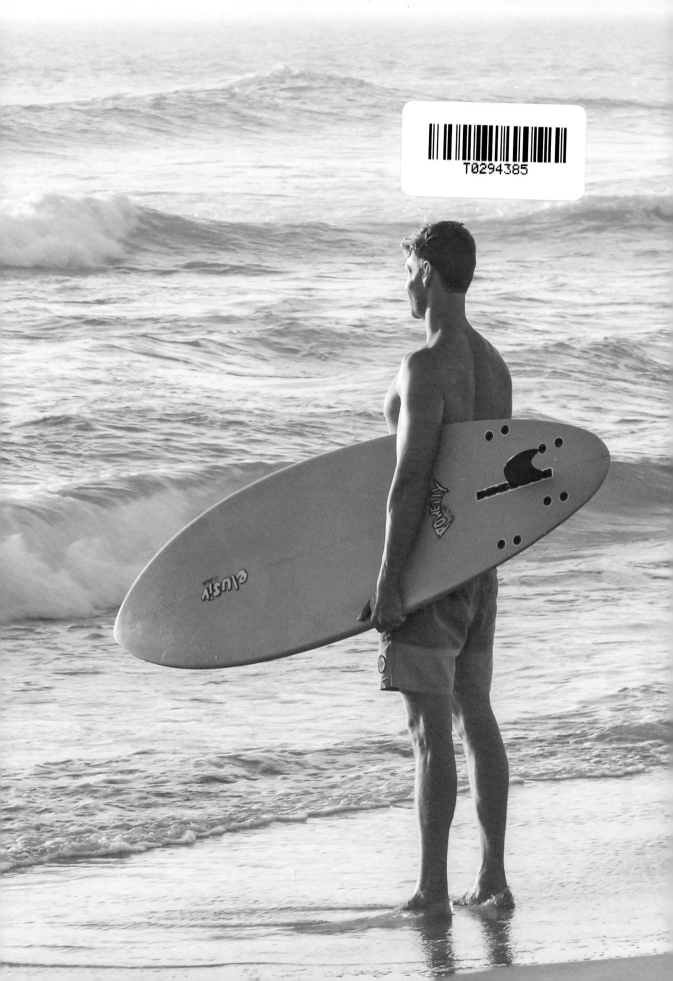

This book is dedicated to all those striving for great health. I hope it empowers you to be the best version of yourself through celebrating real food and enjoying honest cooking.

Eat
CLEAN

& FEEL GREAT
with 100 RECIPES
FOR REAL FOOD
YOU WILL LOVE!

LUKE HINES

plum.

Pan Macmillan Australia

CONTENTS

IT STARTS
with FOOD

HEY GUYS, I've written this book to share my love of food with you and explain why I am so passionate about it. For me, everything starts with food. Clean living, which I advocate, is all about being free and respecting not only your food, but yourself. It's only when you understand the huge role food plays in this, both physically and psychologically, that you'll begin to make the smartest choices possible that will allow you to flourish in all other aspects of your life. With this book I want to help you build a healthy, sustainable relationship with food – the way you think about it, source it, prepare it and enjoy it – which will leave you feeling (and looking) hot, healthy and happy!

I've long had a passion for looking after myself and in turn helping others achieve their goals. Having spent more than ten years as a personal trainer, I know the profound effects food can have on our overall wellbeing, and it was through Channel 7's *My Kitchen Rules* that I could finally share this with a larger audience. Cooking my way to the finals was such an incredible opportunity; not only did I learn a lot about myself, but it was pretty much boot camp for cooking! My knowledge, skills and passion for food grew tenfold throughout this experience, and it has led me to spend more time in the kitchen honing my skills, so that I can inspire others to eat phenomenally delicious food each and every day. With six Clean Living cookbooks already under my belt, I see this book as a wonderful opportunity to reconnect with my current audience, but also to introduce my flavours, philosophy and passion to a whole new set of tastebuds. I am so incredibly excited to share this book with you as it really does reflect my whole ethos around living your best life, through recipes that not only taste epic but can be easily recreated at home.

So, what is it about food that makes me tick? Firstly, I don't believe in restriction, just understanding what you want to eat and why you want to eat it. When you understand this, you'll begin to be able to listen to your body and nourish yourself thoughtfully. Better sleep quality, improved focus, mental clarity and emotional stability are just a few of the other 'life effects' you may experience when cleaning up your act, so to speak. Your tastes and habits may change, and any negativity you may have associated with addictions or cravings should lessen the more you connect with real, nutrient-dense wholefoods. The physical benefits you'll experience will be profound … and all this without counting a single calorie!

I talk a lot about avoiding foods that cause us harm, or inflammation. So what does this mean, exactly? You see, our bodies are designed to defend themselves against outside threats like colds and other viruses in a relatively short-term way – our immune system peaking to deal with these specific threats and then returning to a resting baseline when the job is done. During this resting baseline period, our immune systems fulfil the vitally important role of repairing and maintaining serious body structures. The problem we face is that chronic systemic inflammation can be triggered by certain food choices, specifically the ones I avoid in this book (dairy, grains and refined sugar).

This inflammation is essentially a full-body, long-term up-regulation of immune system activity. Our systems become overloaded by working too hard, too often, and are therefore less effective at doing things like healing other things going on in our bodies. Chronic systemic inflammation is at the heart of an endless number of lifestyle diseases and conditions, such as asthma, heart disease, diabetes and obesity. By following a clean-living lifestyle you will be giving your body the best possible chance of reducing this systemic inflammation.

I'm not going to kid you that taking the leap to following a clean-living lifestyle won't require a bit of a change to the way that you do things, but preparation can be the key to your success. Trust me, it is so worth it, you will thank yourself and wonder why you didn't do it sooner! My advice is to be as organised as possible with your shopping, prepping and cooking. Sit down and pick your favourite recipes to cook. Give yourself plenty of time to stock the correct ingredients, and create a really fun environment to cook in. Don't rush yourself – embrace your creativity and explore the different flavours. Cooking should be fun and exciting. Make it something you really look forward to each day.

You might be wondering at this point what's in store, so let me tell you a little more about what to expect … and get your mouth watering. I've worked hard to pack this book full of my best, most delicious recipes that'll have you buzzing with life and positivity. There's something here for everyone and every occasion – whether you're after a cracking start to the morning for a workday, a lazy brunch, a pre-workout kickstart, a delicious dinner or even your favourite takeaway! Before you know it, you'll be cooking and creating meals that not only look and taste incredible, but are good for you too.

I have used the most nutrient-dense, real foods in each dish, so that eating healthily doesn't mean you skimp on flavour or can't treat yourself to the food you love. Flicking through these pages you'll see there are quite a few sweet treats, which might surprise you. Don't worry, they're all good – I believe that if you are going to indulge, celebrate and enjoy the decadent things in life then they may as well be packed full of the healthiest ingredients on the planet!

For me personally, the positive effects of good food on my health and happiness have been phenomenal. I hope you experience the same life-changing benefits, because life doesn't have to be complicated, and nor does our health. By finding synergy between what we eat, how we move, feeling great and resting, we allow ourselves to flourish. And if we can find a way to incorporate food and lifestyle into one positive, easy, daily routine then we are well on our way to living our lives in the best possible way.

WHAT DOES IT MEAN TO EAT CLEAN?

I want you to think of clean living as a sustainable, long-term approach to living your best possible life by celebrating the most phenomenal tasting, nutrient-dense foods available to us. Essentially, what my recipes are here to do is press the 'reset' button on your health and wellness, creating a happier and healthier you. My food philosophy is loosely based on a paleo or primal way of eating. Now, I say loosely because there are many different levels and interpretations of paleo, so I want to be clear that, for me, it is about being aware of what works for you. I personally feel fantastic when I eliminate grains, dairy and refined sugars from my lifestyle, whereas others can tolerate them no problem. It is about listening to your body, understanding what works for you, making sure your diet is sustainable for your lifestyle and then creating delicious recipes that echo your beliefs. This book contains a plethora of delicious recipes, not only for those who follow a paleo lifestyle, but for those who identify as clean eaters, gluten free, lactose free, sugar quitters, pescetarians, vegetarians, vegans, pagans and, of course, those who just love clean treats.

It's simple, really: celebrate and embrace the foods that allow you to live optimally, and eliminate those foods that can cause you harm or inflammation. Feeling and looking good should come easy, and I want your health and vitality to increase with minimal effort. By embracing my clean-living philosophy, you will increase your energy, lose weight and feel happier and healthier than ever before. How? Well, when we celebrate foods that nourish and nurture our insides, we cultivate an abundance of wellbeing. The sooner we understand that what we consume has a profound effect on our body, the sooner we can understand the best choices when it comes to looking after ourselves through phenomenal food.

INTUITIVE EATING

Much like other aspects of our life where we should follow our gut instinct and listen to our hearts, I believe that when it comes to nourishing ourselves, we should learn to become intuitive eaters and listen to what our bodies want or need. I don't believe we should ever have to count calories, restrict ourselves or even force ourselves to consume anything we don't want to. As soon as you tune in to how your body is working and what types of food make you thrive, you'll find yourself well on the path towards eating intuitively.

When following a clean-living lifestyle, you'll notice that you only eat when you are hungry, and naturally stop when you are full. That's because all of the ingredients we use are about celebrating good health the natural way, and when you begin eating real food, your body responds really positively.

Easy ways to keep it clean

- Keep clear of processed foods
- Embrace and celebrate nutrient-dense wholefoods
- Avoid or limit your intake of grains, dairy, gluten and refined sugar
- Eat when you're hungry and stop when you're full
- Listen to your body and eat intuitively
- Support and consume well-sourced ethical and sustainable protein from land and sea animals
- Choose local, fresh, seasonal produce wherever possible
- Embrace good-quality sources of natural dietary fat
- Promote optimal gut health with bone broths and fermented vegetables
- Be happy. Thinking positively about the changes you're making to your lifestyle makes them easier to stick to

The TIPS, TRICKS and NEED-TO-KNOWS

This is a favourite little section of mine. It's a basic guide to how some of the recipes will work, the ingredients I like to use, what equipment you might find helpful and how to make cooking an enjoyable and rewarding part of your day. I want this lifestyle to be as sustainable as possible for you, so that you see lifelong changes. Living well means committing to a few simple lifestyle choices that I aim to simplify and explain throughout this book. Starting right here, so listen up, legends.

- All oven temperatures listed are for fan-forced ovens. If you are using a conventional oven, the rough rule of thumb is to add 10–20°C to the recommended temperature. Every oven behaves differently, so factor in your knowledge of your own oven. The temperatures provided here are a guide only.

- All my recipes are gluten free, grain free, dairy free and refined sugar free. Whether you have an allergy or not to any of these ingredients, I believe we live to our full potential when we embrace the most nutrient-dense foods on the planet and eliminate those, such as the above, that can cause inflammation.

- I choose ethical and sustainable protein sources from land and sea animals. I highly recommend you do the same for optimal health and wellbeing – not only for ourselves but for the environment too. Poultry should be free range, beef grass fed, pork free range and hormone and nitrate free, and seafood sustainable and line caught if possible. If we expect a happy life we should respect the lives of animals, if we choose to eat them.

- DIY! Clean living is about taking your health into your own hands. We waste so much money buying packet sauces and pre-made stocks and condiments. Learning to make your own is a huge money-saver. Not only will the finished product be better for you, it will taste awesome.

- Cook cheaper cuts of meat. Slow cooking tougher cuts like shoulders, shanks, trotters, hocks and oxtail results in a super-tasty, melt-in-your-mouth experience. You will save money at the register while expanding your cooking repertoire.

- I always soak my nuts. I mean, who doesn't these days, right? What I mean by this is that I activate them before using them in my recipes. This activating process removes naturally occurring chemicals known as enzyme inhibitors that can interfere with our digestive system, preventing us from digesting and absorbing the nutrients we need. Simply soak your nuts for up to 24 hours then, using either a dehydrator or a very low oven, dry them out to make them crunchy again. Not only are they super delicious, they're a totally nutrient-dense snack.

- I'm all about keeping things in their most natural state, which is why I use raw cacao when it comes to anything chocolate-related. Raw cacao is derived from the cacao bean and is simply chocolate in its most pure state. Packed full of vitamins and minerals, this antioxidant-rich superfood is truly where it's at if you want to look and feel great.

- Raw honey, maple syrup and coconut nectar are by far my picks of the bunch when it comes to sweeteners. For me, it is about having a safe, moderate amount of naturally occurring sugars in their most natural state. So even though my treats aren't necessarily an everyday staple, they are certainly the healthiest way to reward yourself.

- Where possible, use organic, seasonal fruit and vegetables. Not only will you avoid harmful pesticides and chemicals, you will be supporting local farmers and an industry that needs all the love it can get.

- Cooking is about trusting your instincts and going with your gut! Pay attention to the balance of flavours among sweet, salty, bitter, sour and umami (the perfect savouriness). None of my recipes are set in stone, so be flexible and, most importantly, have fun.

- If there is one thing I learnt on *My Kitchen Rules* it is to never forget to season. There is something incredible about what a simple sprinkle of salt can do to elevate a dish. #saltfiend right here.

- Keep wastage to a minimum in the kitchen. If you have a fridge full of vegetables that have been there for a while and are looking a bit sad, don't throw them out. Use them to make a stock, or you can finely chop them to create a delicious vegetable soup.

- Be prepared with a well-stocked pantry. By having a good stable of basics, you'll always be able to whip up something quick and easy. And remember, it is often when we are unprepared that we make poorer food choices.

- Have some good-quality, airtight glass containers, jars and bottles on hand for safe food storage. Whether it is for leftovers, nut milks or broths, it is great to have suitable food storage on hand to maximise freshness and minimise waste.

- We all make mistakes! Honestly, I've gone from reality TV contestant to cookbook author and healthy cook and I'm still learning, so don't be afraid to stuff up. There's always tomorrow night's meal.

- Most importantly, have fun and smile. I want you to have a phenomenal time creating all of the recipes in this book. Share them with your family, friends and loved ones, and celebrate life. What's not to be happy about when we are sharing good food with others?

EQUIPMENT

I like to keep things pretty simple when it comes to equipment, so here is my ideal list of items that will make your life in the kitchen a whole lot easier.

BAKEWARE

Be sure to have a number of baking tins on hand, including muffin and loaf tins and deep baking trays. You don't have to go out and buy them all at once, but perhaps treat yourself each time you try one of my recipes that requires something you don't yet have.

BLENDER

A good-quality blender is fantastic for making all of my smoothies, shots and elixirs. Simple to use and a breeze to clean, a good blender is your best bet for achieving the consistency and flavour you're after.

CHOPPING BOARDS

Easy to clean, sturdy and solid, I swear by a number of big, good-quality, wooden chopping boards. I like to have at least two for different types of foods: one for meat, poultry and seafood, and another for fresh fruit, vegetables, nuts and seeds.

FOOD PROCESSOR

A powerful food processor is a must. You'll end up using it for everything from pastry to crumbs, crusts and desserts. Sometimes my recipes call for a full-size food processor and other times I simply use a hand-held blender or mixer. A small hand-held kit with whisk attachments can also come in handy.

GOOD-QUALITY CHEFS KNIFE

They may be more expensive but they'll last longer and they're much easier to use. And don't forget that a sharp knife is a safe knife. There's a great knife sharpener down at my local markets – find someone near you to stay on point!

GOOD-QUALITY POTS AND PANS

The quality of your pans can make a huge difference to the end result, with better control of temperature and less chance of things sticking and getting burnt on the bottom. There are heaps of options out there for clean, healthy non-stick coatings that are better for you and the environment, so shop around.

MANDOLINE

I was first introduced to this little beauty back on *My Kitchen Rules* and since then it has changed my life. So quick – and, be warned, so sharp – you can grate, slice and shred vegetables so they are either paper-thin wafers or thick-cut chips! A mandoline will definitely make your food prep quicker and easier.

THE TOOL BELT

When I refer to my tool belt, I mean that array of miscellaneous items we all need to have: good-quality wooden spoons, spatulas, measuring cups, whisks, mixing bowls and graters, just to name a few. Always read my recipes through first before getting stuck into them so you know you're covered from an equipment point of view.

MUST-HAVE INGREDIENTS FOR YOUR CLEAN-LIVING KITCHEN

Be forward-thinking and organised and you will end up saving cash by not having to make impulse purchases or eat out. Write a list of what you need to stock up on at home and minimise excess purchases throughout the week. The following ingredients appear in lots of my recipes, and I want to share a couple of tips here just in case you're not familiar with their preparation.

APPLE CIDER VINEGAR

I use apple cider vinegar for sauces, dressings and in my broths. Research has shown that when apple cider vinegar is taken before each meal (1–2 teaspoons in a glass of water), it can help improve digestion and is particularly beneficial for people with stomach issues such as reflux, bloating and indigestion.

ARROWROOT (TAPIOCA) FLOUR

Grain and gluten free, I find arrowroot flour perfect for all my baking and crumbing needs. You will see it featured in lots of my recipes due to its wonderful binding and thickening qualities.

AVOCADO OIL

I use avocado oil in a similar way to extra-virgin olive oil: for cold sauces, drizzled over salads or as a side with vegetables. Consuming avocado oil is great for your skin, improves circulatory function and helps to keep hormones in balance. Try switching it up between olive and avocado oil, and play with their different flavour combinations in salad dressings.

AVOCADOS

Avocados are one of the most consumed foods in my house, and for good reason. They contain more potassium than bananas and research has shown people aren't getting enough of that important mineral in their diets. Avocados are one of the fattiest plant foods in existence. The majority of the fat in avocados is the same monounsaturated fatty acid found in olive oil, and is believed to be responsible for some of its beneficial health effects.

BANANAS

The one fruit I always keep on hand (in addition to berries) is the humble banana. Bananas are a wonderfully nutritious and inexpensive food choice with health benefits galore. Their high levels of vitamin B6 help the body make the hormones serotonin and norepinephrine, which influence mood and melatonin production, the latter being what helps regulate the body clock. The unique mix of vitamins, minerals and low-glycaemic carbohydrates in bananas makes them a favourite fruit among athletes.

BEEF, GRASS-FED

Cows are designed to live on a diet of grass, so when they're fed grains and soy products their health and the quality of their meat is compromised. By choosing grass-fed and grass-finished meat (in which the cow has eaten grass for its entire life) you are supporting ethical farming practices with happy cows and high-quality, flavoursome beef. When compared with other types of beef, grass-fed usually has less total fat, more heart-healthy omega-3 fatty acids and more conjugated linoleic acid (a type of fat that's thought to reduce heart disease and cancer risks).

BERRIES

Berries are definitely a staple in my clean-living kitchen. Depending on what I can source, I mix it up between fresh and frozen. Nutritionally speaking all berries are fantastic, so it just comes down to which ones you prefer. What makes berries so special is their high levels of naturally occurring nutrients known as phytochemicals, which help protect cells from damage. They are also a great high-fibre, low-fructose choice of fruit – perfect for those cutting down on sugary foods or managing diabetes.

CACAO

Cacao is basically raw chocolate before all the good stuff has been processed out. With 30 times more antioxidants than blueberries, cacao is an easy and tasty way of getting extra nutrients into your diet. It is important to note that cacao and cocoa are not the same thing. Cocoa is processed cacao, with only a fraction of the nutrients contained in cacao. So if you want serious nutrition, forget cocoa powder or dark chocolate. Stick to raw cacao powder, the more nutrient-dense form of cacao.

COCONUT, DRIED

Flaked, shredded or desiccated, dried coconut makes the perfect addition to a granola and is delicious toasted to top a dessert or used as a crumb when baking or frying. Dried coconut is high in B-complex vitamins, potassium and iron. Make sure when choosing packet varieties that they are unsweetened and contain only 100 per cent dried coconut.

COCONUT BUTTER/PASTE

Coconut butter or paste has a creamy texture and rich flavour. Made from whole ground coconut flesh, it can be used in a range of sweet and savoury dishes. Coconut butter is great for the immune system, as almost half of coconut's fatty-acid profile consists of lauric acid. Apart from mother's milk, there aren't too many other natural sources that have such a high lauric acid content.

COCONUT CREAM

Coconut cream is made the same way as coconut milk but has a higher coconut flesh to water ratio, giving it a thicker, creamier texture. I like to whip coconut cream and use it to top sweet breakfasts and desserts. Read the labels of any store-bought varieties to make sure they haven't sneaked any other ingredients in there. I always choose organic coconut cream in BPA-free cans.

COCONUT FLOUR

Coconut flour is simply ground-up dried coconut flesh. It's a great gluten-free alternative to regular flour and is often used in place of almond meal in recipes, too. It is also a great source of iron, manganese and copper. Keep in mind that coconut flour is very dense and absorbent, so more liquid or eggs are usually required to get the same binding result that almond meal would yield, and to prevent the mixture becoming too crumbly.

COCONUT MILK

There are two types of coconut milk I highly recommend you stock up on: your homemade variety (see recipe on page 35) and the cans you will find at your local supermarket. Both varieties are wonderful for soups, curries, sauces and baking. They are made simply by blending coconut flesh with filtered water, but read the labels of any store-bought varieties to make sure no nasties have been added. I always choose organic coconut milk in BPA-free cans.

COCONUT OIL

I always use cold-pressed organic coconut oil. It is probably the most versatile ingredient in my kitchen, as I use it for frying, baking, smoothies and desserts. Coconut oil is rich in medium-chain triglycerides, which are more easily absorbed into the blood than the long-chain triglycerides in other oils. This means coconut oil is converted to energy much more easily than other oils, helping you feel energised for longer. Try adding it to your morning espresso to experience that 'bulletproof' effect. I recommend choosing organic varieties so you can be sure they don't contain any pesticides or additives.

COCONUT SYRUP

This absolutely delicious low-GI sweetener is made from the liquid sap of the flower of the coconut palm. The sap is placed under heat until most of the water has evaporated, leaving you with pure coconut syrup. Jam-packed with minerals, this syrup has a much darker and richer consistency than honey or maple syrup.

COCONUT WATER

The liquid found in young coconuts is full of electrolytes and magnesium. There are many varieties out there, including fresh, bottled and powdered. Whichever you choose, just make sure there are no added sugars or flavourings. I love coconut water before or after a strenuous workout, as it really replenishes my energy stores. Its sweet flavour also makes it perfect for smoothies and baking.

EGGS, FREE-RANGE

It's best to choose organic free-range eggs – pasture raised where possible – because happy hens produce healthy eggs. And when I say healthy, I mean it! Eggs are one of the cheapest, best-quality sources of protein available. Like quinoa, they contain all the essential amino acids, making them a complete protein. Add to that their omega-3s and high levels of vitamin B2 and you have the perfect meal.

GARLIC

A member of the onion family, this health-boosting bulb is so versatile in the kitchen. Garlic has been shown to be an anti-inflammatory agent and has anti-bacterial and anti-viral properties due to its high vitamin C content. For optimal health benefits, most research recommends eating garlic raw or lightly cooked, but if the flavour is too strong for you, just add whole cloves to a dish and remove them before serving. As for garlic breath, green tea is a great natural remedy.

GHEE

Ghee is a clarified butter commonly used in South Asian cuisines. It is gaining popularity in the paleo community for its high fat content and stability at high cooking temperatures. Ghee is rich in butyric acid, a short-chain fatty acid that nourishes the cells of the intestines, making it great for digestion. So if you're dealing with any sort of digestive issues and taking that important first step of healing your gut lining, ghee is a great way to go.

HERBS

Not only do fresh and dried herbs add flavour and depth to your food, they are rich in antioxidants too. My favourites are fresh basil to make pesto, flat-leaf parsley for my zesty chimichurri and I couldn't live without ground cumin for my Mexican dishes. Get creative and embrace not only how good they taste but how good they are for you, too!

HONEY, RAW

Raw honey is unpasteurised, meaning none of its nutrients have been destroyed by heating and processing. What I love about raw honey is its anti-viral, anti-bacterial and anti-fungal properties. It can promote body and digestive health, is a powerful antioxidant, strengthens the immune system, eliminates allergies and is an excellent natural remedy for skin wounds and all types of infections.

MAPLE SYRUP

Maple syrup is by far my preferred sweetener due to its luscious golden colour, incredible rich flavour and lower fructose content than honey. It doesn't hurt that it's super high in iron, calcium, zinc and potassium, too. When choosing a store-bought variety, make sure the ingredients state it is 100 per cent pure maple syrup and not the imitation product, which contains flavourings and refined sugars.

NUT BUTTERS

Made from ground raw nuts, these oily spreads make a great substitute for regular butter and store-bought toppings and conserves. Full of good fats, fibre and protein, nut butters can be used in smoothies, baking, as a breakfast spread and more. You can make your own by placing raw nuts in a powerful food processor and blending until they form a thick gooey consistency. Make sure you activate them first!

NUT MEAL (FLOUR)

Nut meal is a staple in my house as a gluten-free flour alternative used in baking, crumbing and cooking. My favourite varieties are almond and macadamia meal, which I use to make bread, batter and clean gluten-free desserts. You can make your own by placing raw nuts in a powerful food processor and blending until they form a fine powder.

NUT MILK

Nut milk is my go-to dairy alternative for smoothies, coffees and baking. My favourites are almond and macadamia, as they are the creamiest in my opinion. Loaded with good fats, magnesium and calcium, nut milks are simple to make and taste delicious. Stick to homemade nut milks as store-bought varieties often have added sweeteners, thickening agents and vegetable oils. Head to page 34 for my easy recipe.

OLIVE OIL, EXTRA-VIRGIN

I don't often cook with extra-virgin olive oil because it can go rancid at high temperatures and lose some of its wonderful health benefits, but when it comes to using it cold as a dressing, I simply can't get enough of it. Perfect for strengthening your immune system, extra-virgin olive oil is very high in antioxidants. I'll let you in on another little secret: it may even help with your sex life. You see, olive oil boosts circulation to all areas of the body, including those hard to reach erogenous zones.

PEPPERCORNS

Not only does cracked black pepper add flavour and depth to a dish, it also aids your digestion. Black pepper stimulates the tastebuds in such a way that an alert is sent to the stomach to increase hydrochloric acid secretion, thereby improving digestion. Hydrochloric acid is necessary for the digestion of proteins and other food components in the stomach, so get cracking!

PORK, FREE-RANGE AND NITRATE-FREE

It's important to support ethical farming practices when it comes to purchasing pork products. Always choose free-range, antibiotic-free, hormone-free and nitrate-free pork where possible. When a pig has been eating a natural diet, the meat quality has a very healthy omega-3 to omega-6 ratio, but when a pig is placed on an unnatural diet of corn and/or soy meal, the omega 6s, which are inflammatory to humans, go through the roof.

POULTRY, FREE-RANGE

To avoid any added hormones and chemicals, while at the same time making sure the chickens you eat were able to roam free and eat a natural diet, you need to make smart and ethical purchasing decisions. You'll find phrases like 'pasture-raised', 'pastured', 'free-range' and 'cage-free' on chicken meat packaging, but labelling laws allow products to display these terms even if the chickens spend little or no time outdoors in a pasture setting. Talk to your grocer, local butcher or the chicken farmer and find out how the animals were actually raised before purchasing.

QUINOA

While I could've parked quinoa with Seeds above right, I believe this guy needs his own little write-up. What I love about quinoa is its very high protein content, making it a perfect nutrition source for vegetarians and vegans. In fact, it is one of the only plant-based protein sources that contains all of the essential amino acids (essential meaning the body cannot create them, therefore we need them from a food source). Quinoa is incredibly versatile and can be used across a range of sweet and savoury dishes. See page 44 for my foolproof cooking technique!

SALT, PINK OR ROCK

I recommend replacing any refined table salt with pink or rock salt. These unrefined salts are full of beneficial minerals, which help regulate water content throughout the body, promote healthy pH balance in your cells and can even help reduce signs of ageing.

SEAFOOD, SUSTAINABLE, LINE-CAUGHT OR RESPONSIBLY FARMED

Put simply, 'sustainable seafood' is fish or shellfish that reaches our plates with minimal impact upon fish populations and the wider marine environment. It's not just the numbers of fish left in the ocean that matters, it's the way in which the fish are caught, the impact on the sea floor and other marine wildlife, and how fishing affects the healthy and natural functioning of marine ecosystems.

SEEDS

Seeds are full of nutritional goodness, with incredible flavour to back them up. Pumpkin seeds, flaxseeds and sunflower seeds are some of my faves, but the stand-outs for me are chia seeds. This ancient Aztec staple has become the world's latest superfood sensation, and for good reason! They're loaded with fibre, protein and omega-3 and can be beneficial for weight management, longer-lasting energy, healthy joints, heart and brain health, and inflammation.

SPICES

Some spices have more disease-fighting antioxidants than some fruits and vegetables, so although spices are small, they pack a mean punch. Cinnamon helps lower blood sugar, turmeric can inhibit the growth of cancer cells and paprika has anti-inflammatory properties.

STEVIA

Made from a South American herb, stevia has become increasingly popular in recent years due to its ability to sweeten without affecting blood-sugar levels. With links being drawn between excess sugar consumption and weight gain, many people are now using stevia as a way to decrease calories and body fat. You only need to use it sparingly (it's very sweet), but for anyone wanting to avoid fructose altogether this is a great option.

VANILLA PODS

If I could add these to every recipe I would, and you'll see in most of my breakfast and dessert recipes that I do! Simply make a small incision down one side of the pod, split it open and scrape out the seeds to use in your cooking. When using vanilla in recipes the pod is where it's at: none of this processed and sweetened flavouring or chemically produced essence.

VEGETABLES, FERMENTED

Fermentation techniques have been around for a very long time, mainly as a means to preserve food when refrigeration wasn't available. Today, though, we are rediscovering fermented foods because not only do they taste amazing, they're a great way to consume probiotics – the good bacteria that help promote a healthy gut environment.

VEGETABLES, LOCAL AND SEASONAL

Fresh produce from your region doesn't need to travel weeks across the country (or world) to get to you, meaning it can be picked for taste, not transport. Fruits and vegetables start to lose nutrients immediately after they are harvested, so the freshest produce is the best produce. Plus, shopping at local farmers' markets connects us with the people who live around us and supports the farmers who grow our food.

SHOTS
and ELIXIRS
PAGE 20-23

SMOOTHIES, SHOTS and ELIXIRS

Liquid hits for immunity, energy and recovery

TURMERIC
LATTE
PAGE 19

Kickstart your health with these epic concoctions.

Your new best friend each morning.

TURMERIC LATTE

Made with a combination of turmeric and almond milk – and a source of good fats – this Ayurvedic drink is a warming, free-radical fighting start to your day. Try swapping out your regular morning coffee for it.

Heat a saucepan over medium–low heat. Add the almond milk and, as it begins to warm, whisk in the remaining ingredients until well combined. Continue to heat, whisking gently, until the desired temperature is reached. Pour into two cups or glasses and sprinkle over a little extra cinnamon to serve.

SERVES 2

500 ml (2 cups) Vanilla Almond Milk (see page 34)

2 teaspoons ground turmeric

1 teaspoon ground ginger

1 teaspoon ground cinnamon, plus extra to serve

2 teaspoons maple syrup

2 tablespoons coconut oil, melted

What I love ...

It is common for our bodies to lack sufficient amounts of curcuminoids, the antioxidant compounds found in turmeric, due to their low solubility in water. The coconut oil here helps them to be absorbed and successfully deliver their benefits to the body.

FLU-FIGHTER SHOT

Feeling run down, tired and like you might be on the verge of a cold or flu? If the answer is yes, you have to check out this incredible fiery little concoction. Both the orange and lemon are great sources of vitamin C, the ginger has anti-inflammatory properties and the black pepper helps with the absorption of the turmeric, so that your body can get the full benefits of it. Boost your immunity by having this flu-fighting juice shot in the morning.

1 lemon, peeled

1 orange, peeled

2.5 cm piece of ginger, peeled

2 garlic cloves, peeled

1 teaspoon honey

½ teaspoon ground turmeric

½ teaspoon cayenne pepper

pinch of freshly ground
black pepper

Put the lemon, orange, ginger and garlic through the juicer. Pour into a glass and stir in the remaining ingredients. Drink straight away.

SERVES 1

See a pic of me on page 23

What I love ...

Turmeric is full of active compounds called curcuminoids that have antioxidant properties. They help to support our immune system and can protect our cells from free radical damage.

Tips

To get all the fibre and nutrients available, I recommend juicing the lemon and orange whole, but if that isn't possible just squeezing them will do. Simply finely chop the ginger and garlic and add them to the squeezed juices with the rest of the ingredients.

IMMUNITY-BOOSTING ELIXIR

This little elixir is the perfect year-round go-to for staying on top of your health and wellness. While it isn't as strong as my flu-fighter shot (left), it still packs a decent punch and is a great addition to your morning routine. I've included garlic here because of its incredible track record as an immune system booster – the lemon and lime should mask some of its strong taste.

3 carrots
2 lemons, peeled
1 lime, peeled
2 garlic cloves, peeled
2.5 cm piece of ginger, peeled

Put all the ingredients through the juicer, serve straight up and enjoy.

SERVES 1

See a pic of me on page 22

What I love ...

Carrots are full of the important antioxidants beta-carotene and vitamin A, which play a vital role in supporting your immune system.

If you don't have a juicer you can put all the ingredients in a blender and whiz them together until they become a fine, drinkable pulp. Just add a few dashes of water or coconut water to loosen everything up a little before drinking.

ABC LIVER CLEANSE

This great little liver-cleansing concoction of mine earns its name from its three key ingredients: apple, beetroot and carrot. The earthy flavour of the beetroot can be hard for some, so I have added the lemon and lime to give everything a bit of a fresh zing!

4 green apples
2 beetroot, peeled
4 carrots
1 lemon, peeled
1 lime, peeled

Put all the ingredients through the juicer. Pour into a glass and enjoy.

SERVES 1

See a pic of me on page 22

To deliver the maximum health benefits, along with optimum taste, it is best to juice at the time of consumption. Pre-preparing juice can result in the ingredients oxidising and a loss of freshness and flavour.

IMMUNITY-
BOOSTING
ELIXIR
PAGE 21

ABC LIVER
CLEANSE
PAGE 21

Mix up your mornings
by trying a different
recipe each day.

Feeling tired or run
down? Not for long
with this potent shot!

FLU-FIGHTER
SHOT
PAGE 20

CUCUMBER and MINT GREEN SMOOTHIE

This is a refreshing take on the typical green smoothie, with the additions of celery, cucumber and mint giving it a fantastic light, clean taste. If you're running short on time in the morning, try whizzing one of these babies up – jam-packed with wonderful vitamins and minerals, it's a great way to start your day.

2 Lebanese cucumbers

1 green apple

2 celery stalks

75 g (about 1 cup) kale, stalks removed and leaves torn

2 teaspoons greens supplement powder

1 large handful of mint leaves, plus extra to serve

1 lemon, peeled

125 ml (½ cup) coconut water, plus extra if necessary

4 ice cubes, plus extra to serve

Place all the ingredients in a food processor and whiz everything together until smooth (if it's a bit thick for your liking, loosen it up with some more coconut water). Pour into a tall glass filled with ice and serve with a few extra mint leaves.

SERVES |

I love using greens supplement powder in my smoothies due to the phenomenal levels of nutrients they contain. Just 2 teaspoons of a greens powder that includes greens such as the algae spirulina can offer you the antioxidant equivalent of ten servings of broccoli.

CACAO and RASPBERRY SMOOTHIE

Looking for something sweet without the sugar overload? Well, this smoothie is just that! It's perfect for pre- or post-workout, or even just as an afternoon pick-me-up. A stimulating smoothie that will enliven the senses.

250 ml (1 cup) Vanilla Almond Milk (see page 34)

125 g (1 cup) raspberries, fresh or frozen

1 tablespoon cacao powder

1 tablespoon maple syrup (optional)

4 ice cubes (optional)

1 tablespoon shredded coconut

Put the almond milk, raspberries, cacao, maple syrup (if using) and ice (if using) in a high-speed blender and blitz until smooth. Sprinkle over the shredded coconut to serve. Enjoy!

SERVES |

Raspberries are rich in vitamins, antioxidants and fibre, which makes them not only a delicious addition to this smoothie but a healthy one at that. The raspberries' tartness is balanced out by the bitter taste of cacao, which also provides the minerals magnesium, iron and potassium.

CUCUMBER and
MINT GREEN
SMOOTHIE

CACAO and
RASPBERRY
SMOOTHIE

STRAWBERRY and GINGER LEMONADE

This delicious lemonade has long summer days written all over it. It's perfect for when you're craving a sweet, refreshing drink, while the combination of fresh strawberries and lemon juice gives it a huge vitamin C punch.

150 g (1 cup) strawberries, hulled

250 ml (1 cup) freshly squeezed lemon juice (about 10 lemons)

1 litre (4 cups) filtered water

170 g (½ cup) honey

3 cm piece of ginger (about 35 g), peeled and finely sliced

ice cubes, to serve

lemon slices, to serve

Blend the strawberries in a food processor to form a smooth puree.

Place a medium saucepan over medium–high heat and add the lemon juice, water, honey, ginger and pureed strawberries. Bring the mixture to the boil, then reduce the heat to low and simmer, stirring continuously, until everything is well combined.

Transfer to the refrigerator and leave for 1–2 hours to chill. Serve with ice and freshly sliced lemon.

MAKES 1.25 LITRES (5 CUPS)

What I love ...

It is claimed that the health benefits of vitamin C may include protection against immune system deficiencies, cardiovascular disease and even wrinkles.

PEANUT BUTTER
and JELLY
SMOOTHIE

BANANA and
STRAWBERRY
THICK SHAKE

BANANA and STRAWBERRY THICK SHAKE

This is one of my go-to quick and easy post-workout shakes. I like to add some plant-based protein powder to this when enjoying it after training, but I leave that completely up to you.

1 small banana, frozen if possible

150 g (1 cup) strawberries, frozen if possible

125 ml (½ cup) Vanilla Almond Milk (see page 34)

1 vanilla pod, split and scraped

1 tablespoon chia seeds

4 ice cubes

2 tablespoons protein powder (optional)

fresh strawberries, to serve

Blitz all the ingredients in a high-speed blender until smooth. Garnish with fresh strawberries and serve.

SERVES 1

What I love ...

As well as being a good source of protein, chia seeds are made up of a whopping 65 per cent omega-3 fatty acids, which are great for our overall wellbeing.

The reason I love using frozen bananas and berries is that they make the shake awesomely thick. Don't forget to peel your bananas before freezing them though, as the skin will not come off afterwards. I like to chop them up into small ready-to-use chunks before placing them in the freezer.

PEANUT BUTTER and JELLY SMOOTHIE

A little nod to my regular travel to the United States, the peanut butter and jelly sandwich – or PB & J as it is affectionately known over there – is a sandwich that includes a layer each of peanut butter and jelly (jam) between two slices of bread. This famous American combination of flavours is a favourite of mine and turning it from a high-sugar sandwich into a healthy smoothie was surprisingly easy. I hope you love it!

½ banana, frozen if possible

70 g (½ cup) mixed berries, fresh or frozen

250 ml (1 cup) Vanilla Almond Milk (see page 34)

2 tablespoons peanut butter

4 ice cubes (optional)

crushed peanuts, to serve

Combine all the ingredients in a high-speed blender and blitz until smooth. Garnish with a sprinkling of crushed peanuts. Drink up!

SERVES 1

To make this healthy smoothie into a tasty paleo treat, simply swap the peanut butter for almond or cashew butter instead.

Perfect for your post-workout nutrition hit, or simply just because.

COCONUT and VANILLA PRE-WORKOUT SHAKE
PAGE 32

MOREISH MINT
SLICE SHAKEDOWN
PAGE 32

ROCKY ROAD
RECOVERY
PAGE 33

COCONUT and VANILLA PRE-WORKOUT SHAKE

I love to drink this healthy shake as my pre-workout energy hit. The majority of the energy in this recipe comes from good-quality forms of fat, especially those found in coconuts – coconut oil is easily used by the body as energy, and I find it great when it comes time for training.

250 ml (1 cup) Vanilla Almond Milk (see page 34)
2 tablespoons shredded coconut or fresh coconut flesh
1 vanilla pod, split and scraped
1 teaspoon maca powder
1 tablespoon coconut oil, melted
1 teaspoon ground cinnamon
4 ice cubes
1 teaspoon cacao nibs, to serve

Combine all the ingredients except the cacao nibs in a high-speed blender and blitz until smooth. Sprinkle over the cacao nibs and enjoy.

SERVES 1

See a pic of me on page 30

What I love ...

Commonly known as Peruvian ginseng, maca is an incredible superfood. It boosts energy, vitality and increases your libido, so should have you bouncing off the (bedroom) walls ...

MOREISH MINT SLICE SHAKEDOWN

I have really fond memories of coming home from school and my mum giving me a classic chocolate mint slice biscuit for afternoon tea. Well, 20 years down the track and, although I don't indulge in sweet treats of that kind anymore, I have recreated that awesome taste in this smoothie – together with beneficial nutrients that pack a punch.

250 ml (1 cup) Vanilla Almond Milk (see page 34)
2 large handfuls of mint leaves, plus extra to serve
1 banana, frozen
1 tablespoon cacao powder
1 tablespoon almond butter
½ avocado

Put all the ingredients in a high-speed blender and whiz together until smooth. Pour into a glass, finish with the extra mint leaves and off you go.

SERVES 1

See a pic of me on page 31

What I love ...

The aroma of mint activates the salivary glands in our mouths as well as glands which secrete digestive enzymes, thereby facilitating digestion.

ROCKY ROAD RECOVERY

Rocky road is such a popular treat that I wanted to give you guys that same phenomenal taste without any of the processed ingredients. So just shut your eyes and imagine that distinctive dark chocolate, marshmallow and nut combination in each and every sip of this incredible smoothie. Due to the sugars from the berries and dates in this one, I like to use it as a recovery drink after a strenuous workout.

Blitz together the almond milk, cacao powder, berries, hazelnuts, dates, shredded coconut and ice cubes in a high-speed blender until smooth. Garnish with the fresh raspberries and a few extra crushed hazelnuts. Serve and enjoy!

SERVES 4

See a pic of me on page 31

250 ml (1 cup) Vanilla Almond Milk (see page 34)

1 tablespoon cacao powder

70 g (½ cup) mixed berries, fresh or frozen

75 g (½ cup) hazelnuts, plus extra to serve

2 medjool dates, pitted

2 tablespoons shredded coconut

4 ice cubes

fresh raspberries, to serve

VANILLA ALMOND MILK

I love this dairy-free alternative to regular cow's milk. From starting my day with it in my morning coffee, to utilising it in so many of my recipes, I love having nut milk on hand.

155 g (1 cup) almonds, soaked in water for at least 8 hours

1 litre (4 cups) filtered water

1 vanilla pod, split and scraped

pinch of sea salt

Drain the soaked nuts and rinse them really well. Place all the ingredients in a high-speed blender and blend for 2–3 minutes or until nice and creamy.

Line a bowl with either a nut milk bag or a piece of muslin, so that the fabric hangs over the edge of the bowl.

Pour the blended nut and water mixture into the bowl. Pick up the edges of the bag or muslin and squeeze out all the milk (like milking the nuts, so to speak!). Keep the leftover pulp to use in your baking.

Store the milk in an airtight container in the fridge for up to 4 days, being sure to shake well before each use.

MAKES 1.25 LITRES (5 CUPS)

See a pic of me on page 37

Tips

To make a cacao nut milk, add 1 tablespoon ground cinnamon, 125 g (1 cup) cacao powder and 100 g pitted medjool dates that have been soaked in boiling water for 10 minutes to the blender with the other ingredients. Try experimenting with different types of nuts and mixing nut milks too – I personally love the combination of macadamia and cashew milk.

Be mindful of store-bought nut milks, as they often contain less than ideal ingredients. Making your own is cheaper and way more delicious.

HOMEMADE COCONUT MILK

This is a quick and easy recipe that can be used in addition to, or as a replacement for, the almond milk in many of my recipes. Much lighter than the canned stuff, this coconut milk is perfect for your warm drinks, smoothies and curries.

Pour the filtered water into a saucepan over medium heat and bring to a simmer. Remove from the heat and pour into a blender. Add the shredded coconut, vanilla seeds and salt and blend or pulse on high for 2–5 minutes, or until the liquid becomes thick and creamy.

Line a colander with two large layers of muslin and place over a large bowl. Pour the coconut milk through the lined colander, then pick up the edges of the muslin and squeeze as much liquid as possible out of the coconut through the colander.

Store the coconut milk in an airtight container in the refrigerator for up to 3–4 days, being sure to give it a bit of a shake before use as the solids can settle on the bottom.

MAKES 1.25 LITRES (5 CUPS)

See a pic of me on page 36

1 litre (4 cups) filtered water
120 g (2 cups) shredded coconut
1 vanilla pod, split and scraped
pinch of sea salt

HOMEMADE
COCONUT MILK
PAGE 35

Save your leftover
nut pulp and use it in
your baking.

VANILLA
ALMOND MILK
PAGE 34

BACON and
EGG BREKKIE
MUFFINS
PAGE 50

APPLE and
CINNAMON
BIRCHER MUESLI
PAGE 44

OUT the DOOR

Nourishing breakfasts
to grab and go

You don't want to
miss these babies.

CACAO
BREAKFAST
BITES
PAGE 49

CHIA SEED PUDDING with RASPBERRY and LIME COULIS

This is one of those incredible recipes that you can get ready the night before, making your breakfast quick, simple and, most of all, delicious! When soaked overnight, chia seeds become gelatinous, giving this little baby a pudding-like consistency, though unlike a real pudding this is actually a phenomenal source of antioxidants and fibre.

Put the chia seeds, almond milk and maple syrup or honey in a bowl or an airtight container, cover with plastic wrap or a lid and leave to soak overnight in the refrigerator.

To make the coulis, using the back of a fork, mash together the raspberries, maple syrup or honey and lime zest in a bowl. Set aside in the fridge overnight.

When you are ready to enjoy your pudding in the morning, give your chia seed mixture a good stir. Spoon it into bowls or some nice clear glass tumblers, top with the coulis and serve garnished with some fresh mint or lime zest, if you like. Feel free to add a little extra almond or coconut milk when serving, if you like a runnier pudding.

SERVES 2

| 50 g (⅓ cup) chia seeds |
| 250 ml (1 cup) Vanilla Almond Milk or Homemade Coconut Milk (see pages 34 and 35), plus extra to serve (optional) |
| 1 tablespoon maple syrup or honey |
| mint leaves, to serve (optional) |

Raspberry and lime coulis

| 125 g (1 cup) raspberries, fresh or frozen |
| 1 tablespoon maple syrup or honey |
| 1 teaspoon grated lime zest, plus extra to serve (optional) |

What I love ...

Chia seeds contain five times more calcium than milk, making them the perfect non-dairy way to start the day.

This packs up wonderfully in jars and would be a great little surprise for someone at work, so double or triple the quantities I have set out here and stock up for a couple of days' worth of incredible breakfasts and snacks in advance.

TOASTY MAPLE and PECAN GRANOLA

Mmmm, I can taste the cinnamon goodness in this granola just writing the recipe down for you guys. Some traditional granolas are full of processed sugars to bind the ingredients together – the reason I love my version is because it offers a subtle, sweet taste while being filled with my favourite nuts and seeds, making it delicious and really good for you too!

3 tablespoons coconut oil, melted

3 tablespoons maple syrup

200 g (2 cups) pecans, crushed

1 tablespoon shredded coconut

125 g (1 cup) pumpkin seeds

60 g (½ cup) sunflower seeds

1 teaspoon ground cinnamon

To serve

Whipped Coconut Cream
(see page 213)

fresh berries

edible flower petals (optional)

Get started by preheating the oven to 200°C and lining a large baking tray with baking paper.

In a large bowl, combine the coconut oil and maple syrup, then add the pecans, shredded coconut and all the seeds. Mix everything together until all the dry ingredients are well coated in the syrup mixture.

Spread the granola evenly over the baking paper and bake for 20 minutes, or until everything turns nice and golden brown.

Remove the tray from the oven and leave to cool, then add the cinnamon and mix well. Transfer to an airtight container and store for up to 2 weeks. To serve, top with whipped coconut cream and fresh berries – and some edible flower petals if you're feeling extra fancy!

MAKES 10 SERVINGS

What I love ...

Pecans aren't only delicious, they are really good for you too. Pecans are among the most antioxidant-rich nuts and may help prevent the formation of plaque in your arteries.

Add 60 g (½ cup) cacao nibs to your mixture to turn it into a choc-chip breakfast crunch! Now that's how I like to start my day ...

APPLE and CINNAMON BIRCHER MUESLI

This fresh and zesty muesli offers the same amazing bircher taste you've come to know and love but without the gluten or dairy that are present in so many other versions. I love this muesli because you can make a large batch of it at the beginning of the week and enjoy it each morning with no prep time at all, making it perfect for those mornings when you need to run out the door!

200 g (1 cup) quinoa, rinsed

sea salt

3 green apples

3 tablespoons slivered almonds

1 tablespoon coconut flakes, toasted

4 tablespoons Whipped Coconut Cream (see page 213) or coconut yoghurt

160 g (1 cup) blueberries, fresh or frozen

1 teaspoon ground cinnamon

finely grated zest of 1 lime

Bring 375 ml (1½ cups) of water to the boil in a medium–large saucepan with a lid. Add the quinoa and a generous pinch of salt. Return to the boil then immediately put on the lid, reduce the heat to the lowest setting possible and simmer gently for 15 minutes. During this time, do not stir or move the quinoa in any way. Remove the pan from the heat and let stand, still with the lid on, for up to 5 minutes. Remove the lid, gently fluff up the grains with a fork and set aside to cool.

Put two of the apples through a juicer and pour the juice into a large bowl. Grate the remaining apple into the same bowl, discarding the core and pips.

Add 2 cups of the cooled quinoa to the bowl (save the leftovers for a salad) together with the remaining ingredients and mix together well. Leave the mixture to soak for at least 10 minutes before transferring to an airtight container. Store in the fridge for up to 5 days and enjoy at your leisure throughout the week.

SERVES 4

You can play around with the flavours of this recipe really easily by swapping the blueberries for raspberries and the almonds for toasted pistachio nuts. If you prefer your bircher to be less thick, simply stir in some almond milk to make it runnier and creamier.

Take your time, eat
mindfully and fall in
love with food.

CACAO BREAKFAST BITES

These bites are all about enjoying the incredible health benefits of cacao combined with breakfast favourites such as banana and chia seeds. Make a big batch of these on Sunday afternoon and store them in an airtight container in the fridge for the week ahead.

Start by preheating the oven to 180°C. Grease a 12-hole muffin tin with some coconut oil.

Place the eggs, mashed banana, almond butter, coconut oil and vanilla seeds in a large mixing bowl and whiz together with a hand-held blender until well combined. Add the remaining ingredients and whiz again to mix everything together well.

Spoon the mixture evenly into the muffin tin until each of the holes are about two-thirds full.

Bake for 20–25 minutes, or until lightly golden and cooked through. To test, give your chocolatey bites a little touch on top – if they don't sink they're good to go. Remove them from the muffin tin carefully and allow them to cool slightly on a wire rack before devouring.

MAKES 12

5 eggs
4 very ripe bananas, mashed with a fork
125 g almond butter
80 ml (⅓ cup) coconut oil, melted
1 vanilla pod, split and scraped
65 g (½ cup) coconut flour
120 g (1 cup) cacao powder
1 tablespoon chia seeds
2 teaspoons ground cinnamon
½ teaspoon baking powder
pinch of sea salt

What I love ...

Cacao has been proven to be a massive energy and mood booster, which makes it the perfect morning hit – its natural stimulant effect really gives you that extra kick to get you going

Tip

Try scattering a few frozen berries on top before you bake these breakfast bites for a little extra colour and flavour (I personally love using raspberries).

BACON and EGG BREKKIE MUFFINS

I'm a massive fan of vegetable-packed frittatas, so I wanted to find a way to incorporate all that delicious flavour into one easy-to-grab-and-go bite. Introducing the bacon and egg brekkie muffins! Packed full of delicious vegetables, herbs and spices, these take breakfast on the go to the next level. They are great to bake at the start of the week and keep stored in the refrigerator for those busy mornings when you're running out the door. When using chilli in this recipe, make sure you are aware of the heat factor you will be adding. I use the whole chilli, including the membrane and seeds, but this can make it extra spicy, so for a milder heat, remove the membrane and seeds before finely slicing.

300 g zucchini, grated

1 red capsicum, finely diced

½ red onion, finely diced

2 garlic cloves, finely chopped

4 bacon rashers, finely diced

1 long red chilli, finely sliced (optional)

sea salt and freshly ground black pepper

10 eggs

3 tablespoons Vanilla Almond Milk or Homemade Coconut Milk (see pages 34 and 35)

½ bunch of flat-leaf parsley, leaves picked and finely chopped

your favourite sauce or chutney, to serve

Start by preheating the oven to 200°C and greasing a 12-hole muffin tin with coconut oil.

In a bowl combine the zucchini, capsicum, onion, garlic, bacon and chilli (if you like it hot) and mix well with a light seasoning of salt and pepper. Spoon the mixture into the muffin holes and bake for 10 minutes.

Meanwhile, combine the eggs, almond or coconut milk and finely chopped parsley in a bowl and whisk together well until really light and fluffy.

Remove the muffin tin from the oven and pour the egg mixture over the vegetable and bacon mixture almost to the top of each hole. Return to the oven and bake for a further 6 minutes, or until the eggs are completely set. Allow them to cool in the tin for a few minutes, then remove carefully.

Serve covered with your favourite sauce or chutney. These will last in the fridge for 2–3 days if stored in an airtight container.

MAKES 12

This is one of those recipes that you can really apply some creative licence to. Try swapping the bacon for leftover lamb, pork or beef from the night before, mixing it up with different herbs or spices or switching the vegetables around to give you a whole new flavour combination. Or use poached salmon as your protein and add beautiful ingredients like fennel, cherry tomatoes and dill.

GREEN BREAKFAST SALAD with HERBED EGGS

Who said you can't have salad for breakfast? The great thing about this dish is that, due to its cold nature, it doesn't have to be cooked fresh in the morning – it's perfect made the evening before, ready to be grabbed and eaten on the go. Avocados are a great source of good-quality fat that have an amazing way of keeping us feeling satiated for longer, meaning that after this breakfast you won't be reaching for any naughty mid-morning snack.

4 eggs

1 tablespoon finely chopped flat-leaf parsley leaves

1 tablespoon finely chopped coriander leaves

1 tablespoon sesame seeds

1 tablespoon roughly chopped hazelnuts

1 tablespoon roughly chopped cashew nuts

1 tablespoon roughly chopped almonds

1 tablespoon pumpkin seeds

2 large avocados, roughly chopped

1 small handful of kale, stalks removed and leaves finely chopped

2 tablespoons avocado oil

finely grated zest and juice of 1 lemon

sea salt and freshly ground black pepper

Lower the eggs into a saucepan of boiling water, reduce the heat to a simmer and cook for 3–6 minutes depending on how firm you like them – I like mine extra runny so I don't cook them for too long. Drain, then peel off the shells under cold running water. Leave to cool.

Place the parsley, coriander and sesame seeds in a bowl, add the peeled eggs and roll them in the herb mixture to coat them all over. Set aside.

In a separate large bowl, toss together the chopped nuts, pumpkin seeds, avocado and kale until well combined. Dress evenly with the avocado oil and lemon juice, and season with salt and pepper to taste.

Divide the salad between two serving bowls, top with the boiled eggs and garnish with the lemon zest. For extra visual amazingness, cut the boiled eggs in half to allow the yolk to ooze all over the delicious salad before serving.

SERVES 2

If you feel the need to beef this dish up a little, try adding a slice of one of my amazing gluten-free loaves from the Bakery chapter (see pages 81–101). Boiled eggs (in the shell) can be stored in the fridge for up to 1 week, so make up a big batch to have on hand for this breakfast, as well as for snacks throughout the day.

Weekends are perfect
for celebrating the joy
of cooking and sharing
food with others.

SMASHED
AVO with
GOOEY EGGS
PAGE 65

FLUFFY
HOTCAKES with
ZESTY LEMON CURD
PAGE 57

WEEKEND BREAKFAST

Cafe-worthy brunches
without the crowds

CREPES
with ROASTED
STRAWBERRY SAUCE
or HOMEMADE 'NUTELLA'
and COCONUT CRUNCH
PAGE 62

FLUFFY HOTCAKES with ZESTY LEMON CURD

OK, so I might appear to be a strict fitness enthusiast, but I also have a massive sweet tooth. For me, when it comes to indulging, it is about swapping out any ingredients that might not make me look, feel and perform at my best, and replacing them with nutrient-dense equivalents. That's why these fluffy hotcakes are amazing – they have the most incredible texture without any of the naughty ingredients. This is one lazy weekend breakfast I put on repeat!

Preheat the oven to 180°C.

For the lemon curd, place the lemon zest, lemon juice and maple syrup in a saucepan over medium heat. Bring the mixture to a simmer, then remove the pan from the heat and whisk in the arrowroot flour until smooth. Return the pan to the heat and whisk for a further 2–3 minutes, or until the mixture becomes thick, then remove the pan from the heat again and whisk in the butter and egg yolks to form a smooth, sticky sauce. Set aside to cool slightly.

In a large mixing bowl, beat the eggs until they are really light and airy. Add the maple syrup, almond or coconut milk and vanilla seeds and whisk again until really well combined. Steadily add the dry ingredients to the bowl and mix everything together well to form a thick batter, adding a little extra coconut flour if the batter is looking too wet.

Melt 1–2 tablespoons of the coconut oil in a small, ovenproof frying pan over medium heat (you don't want the pan too hot or your hotcakes will burn before they are cooked through). Pour half of the batter into the hot pan and cook for about 2–3 minutes. Transfer the pan to the oven and cook for 10 minutes or until cooked through. To get a nice colour on the top, cook for a further 2 minutes under the grill. Keep warm and repeat with the remaining batter, greasing the pan lightly first to prevent sticking, to make two large hotcakes.

Place the hotcakes on serving plates and spoon over the warm, zesty lemon curd. Serve with the whipped coconut cream or coconut yoghurt (if using) and a sprinkling of coconut flakes.

SERVES 2

9 eggs
2 tablespoons maple syrup
500 ml (2 cups) Vanilla Almond Milk (see page 34) or Homemade Coconut Milk (see page 35)
1 vanilla pod, split and scraped
130 g (1 cup) coconut flour, plus extra if needed
2 teaspoons baking powder
2 teaspoons ground cinnamon
1 teaspoon ground nutmeg
2 teaspoons maca powder
pinch of sea salt
2–4 tablespoons coconut oil
Whipped Coconut Cream (see page 213) or coconut yoghurt, to serve (optional)
20 g (⅓ cup) coconut flakes, lightly toasted, to serve

Zesty lemon curd (makes 360 g)

2 tablespoons finely grated lemon zest
250 ml (1 cup) lemon juice
1 tablespoon maple syrup
2 tablespoons arrowroot flour
150 g unsalted butter or ghee, melted
2 egg yolks

Tips

These bad boys can be frozen and enjoyed later, so make a big batch of them and put them in the kids' lunch boxes! They're great eaten cold. You don't have to waste the egg whites leftover from making the curd – reserve them and add them to your smoothies, or boost your breakfast with an egg white omelette.

QUINOA PORRIDGE with BLUEBERRY COMPOTE

This favourite of mine is the perfect winter warmer – protein-rich quinoa combined with creamy homemade almond milk and the tart, refreshing hit of blueberry compote. It's perfect for those cold weekend mornings when you have a little bit more time to put into your breakfast prep.

50 g (¼ cup) quinoa, rinsed

125 ml (½ cup) Vanilla Almond Milk (see page 34)

125 ml (½ cup) filtered water

1 cinnamon stick

1 tablespoon roughly chopped toasted almonds

Blueberry compote

1 green apple

155 g (1 cup) blueberries

1 tablespoon maple syrup

pinch of ground cinnamon

Place the quinoa, almond milk, filtered water and cinnamon stick in a saucepan. Bring everything to the boil, then reduce to a simmer and cook over low heat, stirring occasionally, for 15 minutes.

While the quinoa is underway, get to work on your blueberry compote. Peel, core and finely dice the apple and place it in a small saucepan over high heat with the rest of the compote ingredients and 2 tablespoons or so of water. Bring to the boil, then reduce the heat to low and simmer for 10 minutes to form a chunky, textured compote. Set aside and leave to cool slightly.

Once the quinoa is cooked, spoon the porridge into two serving bowls, top with the warm compote and scatter over the almonds.

SERVES 2

What I love ...

Quinoa is a low-carbohydrate seed with a very low glycaemic load, which means it releases its energy slowly and helps you maintain steady blood-sugar levels.

If you prefer your compote smooth, give it a quick blitz with a hand-held blender after leaving it to cool.

The best thing to do is
to make a massive batch.

COOK and EAT

When it comes to food, my clean-living philosophy is about embracing and celebrating the most nutrient-dense ingredients on the planet and avoiding or minimising those that cause you harm or inflammation. But I don't believe that adhering to these principles needs to be complicated or that we should compromise on flavour.

I believe preparing food should be one of the most pleasurable parts of your day. For me, it is something I certainly look forward to. Just think about it, you're fortunate enough to be working with the best of what nature has given us to thrive on. Plus, there is something phenomenal about enjoying something your own labour has produced – that awesome moment when you sit down with a grin from ear to ear and can be proud of what you have created. Actually eating the food is another experience in itself – it's a time when we stop everything else that is going on in our day and can immerse ourselves in all that we have in front of us. It is also a time when we can reflect, connect with others and eat mindfully.

Being empowered enough to take your health into your own hands by preparing your own food is one of the greatest things you can do to be the best version of yourself – and it can start all the way back at the farm. Take an interest in where your food comes from, ask about where it is sourced and respect your produce by caring about how it ends up on your plate. This allows you to be the judge of what foods you want to eat, allowing you to thrive and flourish, while nourishing yourself for your particular health and fitness goals. So, legends, get into the kitchen and cook up a storm. Be sure to enjoy the process and make it an integral part of your world.

CREPES with ROASTED STRAWBERRY SAUCE or HOMEMADE 'NUTELLA' and COCONUT CRUNCH

Crepes are a form of thin pancake that originated on the Atlantic coast of France. Now, although my travels haven't taken me that far, I have really fond memories of lemon crepes from the Red Hill markets back when I was a little kid; cold Victorian mornings spent walking around the market, finding warmth and comfort in my little tray of tastiness. Here's my take on this childhood favourite of mine.

65 g (½ cup) arrowroot or tapioca flour

1 tablespoon coconut flour

pinch of sea salt

4 eggs

3 egg whites

250 ml (1 cup) Vanilla Almond Milk (see page 34)

1 tablespoon maple syrup

80–100 ml coconut oil

Roasted strawberry sauce (makes 250 ml/1 cup)

450 g (4 cups) fresh strawberries, hulled and quartered

1 tablespoon maple syrup

Homemade 'nutella' and coconut crunch (makes 125 g)

55 g (½ cup) hazelnut meal

1 tablespoon cacao powder

80 ml (⅓ cup) maple syrup

2 tablespoons Vanilla Almond Milk (see page 34), plus extra if needed

1 tablespoon coconut flakes, toasted, to serve

To make the strawberry sauce, preheat the oven to 180°C and line a baking tray with baking paper. Spread the strawberry pieces evenly over the tray and bake for 20–25 minutes, until soft and juicy. Tip the strawberry pieces into a bowl and stir through the maple syrup with a fork to form a chunky sauce. Set aside.

For the homemade 'nutella', place the hazelnut meal, cacao powder, maple syrup and almond milk in a bowl and blend with a hand-held blender to form a lovely smooth paste. Add a little extra almond milk if you need to loosen it up. Set aside.

Put the arrowroot or tapioca flour, coconut flour and salt in a bowl, and mix together well. In a separate bowl, combine the eggs, egg whites, almond milk and maple syrup. Slowly add the wet ingredients to the dry, whisking all the while to avoid any lumps, until the two are well combined and you have a light, fluffy batter. Alternatively, place all the ingredients in a food processor and pulse until no lumps remain.

Melt 1–2 tablespoons of the coconut oil in a frying pan over medium–high heat, add one-sixth of the batter and spread it out by tilting the pan to ensure it coats the base in an even, thin layer. Cook the crepe for 40 seconds before using a spatula to carefully flip it over. Cook for a further 15 seconds, then remove from the pan and keep warm. Repeat with the remaining crepe mixture, greasing the pan lightly with more coconut oil between pancakes to make sure they don't stick to the pan.

To serve, spread the 'nutella' over the crepes and top with the toasted coconut flakes, or spoon over the strawberry sauce.

MAKES 6 CREPES

The reason I love making my own 'nutella' and strawberry sauce is because so many of the store-bought varieties are full of hidden refined sugars, colours and flavourings – ingredients we don't want to be consuming when living clean. Take your health into your own hands by preparing as many of your own sides and sauces as possible, and see and taste the difference.

The best
breakfast in bed
you can get.

SMASHED AVO with GOOEY EGGS

When I see smashed avocado on a cafe menu my eyes light up as if all my Christmases have come at once. There's something incredibly delicious about these simple flavours at breakfast, which is why I've created this zesty little recipe to put a smile on your dial for the day ahead!

Toast the chia and zucchini hazelnut bread under the grill until nicely golden and crunchy.

Top each slice of toast with the avocado. Halve the boiled eggs lengthways and lay them over the avocado, yolk-side up, then sprinkle over the chia seeds, cumin, paprika and chilli flakes and season with salt and pepper. Serve with lemon wedges for squeezing over the top.

SERVES 2

2 slices of Chia and Zucchini Hazelnut Bread (see page 88)

1 large avocado, mashed

2 eggs, soft-boiled and peeled

1 tablespoon chia seeds

1 teaspoon ground cumin

1 teaspoon sweet paprika

1 teaspoon dried chilli flakes

sea salt and freshly ground black pepper

lemon wedges, to serve

ZUCCHINI and SWEET POTATO HASH with BACON, FRIED EGGS and MACADAMIA RICOTTA

I love to start my day with this breakfast, which has got to be one of my favourites. In fact, just writing this recipe for you guys has got my mouth watering. The combination of the slow-release carbohydrates from the sweet potato together with the good fats from the avocado, bacon and eggs will have you powering through your day and feeling phenomenal.

1 sweet potato, coarsely grated

1 large zucchini, grated

¼ red onion, grated

55 g (½ cup) almond meal

1 tablespoon dried chilli flakes

pinch of sea salt

6 eggs

80 ml (⅓ cup) coconut oil

4 bacon rashers

lemon wedges, to serve

handful of mint leaves, to serve

**Macadamia ricotta
(makes 500 g/1½ cups)**

320 g (2 cups) macadamia nuts

2 tablespoons lemon juice

1 teaspoon sea salt

125 ml (½ cup) filtered water, plus extra if needed

Start by preparing the delicious macadamia ricotta. Put all the ingredients in a food processor and puree to a smooth paste, scraping down the sides with a spatula halfway through to ensure everything gets mixed together well, and adding a little extra water if you need to loosen it up. Set aside.

Now get on with the rest of the dish. In a bowl, combine the sweet potato, zucchini, onion, almond meal, chilli flakes, salt and two of the eggs to form a batter.

Melt the coconut oil in a large frying pan over medium heat. Spoon the sweet potato mixture into the pan in four loose rounds and press down lightly on each to form round fritters. Cook for about 3 minutes on each side until crisp and tender.

Meanwhile, fry the remaining eggs and the bacon in a separate pan until cooked to your liking. Transfer all of the elements to serving plates and accompany with the macadamia ricotta, a few lemon wedges and a scattering of mint leaves. Season and enjoy.

SERVES 2

What I love ...

I love using sweet potatoes because, although they are naturally sweet-tasting, their sugars are slowly released into the bloodstream, helping to ensure a balanced and regular source of energy without the usual blood-sugar spikes linked to fatigue and weight gain.

EGGS BENEDICT with COCONUTTY HOLLANDAISE

Everybody loves a good eggs benedict, so I wanted to give you my version with my clean living spin on it. I've found a way to enjoy the same great taste of hollandaise without the dairy by using coconut oil. Enjoy, legends!

2 teaspoons apple cider vinegar

4 eggs

2 tablespoons coconut oil

120 g baby spinach leaves

4 slices of Coconut Breakfast Loaf (see page 89), toasted

4 slices of smoked salmon

Coconutty hollandaise

2 egg yolks

1 tablespoon lemon juice

3 tablespoons coconut oil, melted

½ teaspoon sea salt

1 tablespoon finely chopped flat-leaf parsley leaves, plus extra leaves to serve

Add the apple cider vinegar to a large saucepan filled with filtered water and bring to the boil. Reduce to a simmer, crack in the eggs and poach for 4–5 minutes, or until the whites are completely cooked. Carefully remove the eggs from the water with a slotted spoon and transfer to paper towel to remove any excess water.

Meanwhile, melt the coconut oil in a large non-stick frying pan over medium heat. Add the baby spinach and sauté until softened. Set aside.

For the coconutty hollandaise, put the egg yolks and lemon juice in a blender and pulse to combine. With the blender running on low, slowly pour in the melted coconut oil, then add the salt and parsley and blend to a smooth, creamy sauce.

To serve, place the spinach on top of the toasted bread and layer with the smoked salmon slices. Top with the poached eggs, generously spoon over the coconut hollandaise sauce and garnish with the extra parsley leaves.

SERVES 2

Also known as eggs royale, this version of eggs benedict can be switched back to the classic by replacing the smoked salmon with ham. I love both flavour combinations – it just depends on what your tastebuds are asking for!

This dish really
enlivens the senses with
the tastes of Mexico!

MEXICAN SCRAMBLED EGGS with CHIMICHURRI

Mexican has got to be one of my favourite cuisines; its extensive use of mouth-tingling herbs and spices really enliven the palate, and I gravitate towards the freshness it offers. That's why I love this great option for breakfast – its bold flavours are certain to start your day with a punch.

Get started by preparing the chimichurri. Put all the ingredients in a food processor and pulse for 10 seconds or so to form a chunky sauce (be careful not to over-pulse at this point, as you don't want it too smooth). Set aside and get going on the scramble.

Melt the coconut oil in a frying pan over medium heat. Add the chorizo, onion, capsicum, garlic and chilli and sauté for 2–3 minutes or until golden and caramelised. Add the tomato and spices and cook for a further 2 minutes, then tip the beaten egg into the pan and cook, gently folding the mixture together as you go, until scrambled to your liking.

Divide the scrambled eggs between two plates, season with salt and serve with lime wedges and a generous helping of the chimichurri.

SERVES 2

The stalks of the parsley and coriander can be used in this chimichurri, so be sure not to waste them. This chimichurri recipe makes more than you'll need here, so store the leftovers in an airtight container for up to 4–5 days in the fridge and enjoy it drizzled over your vegetables, salads and meats over the coming days.

1 tablespoon coconut oil

60 g (¼ cup) diced chorizo

½ red onion, finely diced

½ capsicum, finely diced

1 garlic clove, diced

1 long red chilli, diced

1 small tomato, diced

1 teaspoon sweet paprika

1 teaspoon ground cumin

6 eggs, beaten

sea salt

lime wedges, to serve

Chimichurri
(makes 375 ml/1½ cups)

2 large handfuls of flat-leaf parsley, leaves and stalks

2 large handfuls of coriander, leaves and stalks

3 garlic cloves

1 long red chilli

125 ml (½ cup) extra-virgin olive oil

2 tablespoons apple cider vinegar

juice of 2 lemons

½ teaspoon sea salt

EPIC FENNEL and KALE FRITTATA

This is a fantastic example of simple cooking at its best. Once the vegetables are roasted off, you transfer the pan straight to the oven, delivering incredible flavour by utilising all the juices in the pan as well as making less mess for wash-up time. This recipe is an awesome way to start the day, but also makes the best lunch or dinner.

1 fennel bulb, finely sliced

1 onion, finely sliced

2 tablespoons black olives, pitted and roughly chopped

2 tablespoons coconut oil, melted

200 g (2 cups) kale, stalks removed and leaves finely chopped

2 garlic cloves, grated

8 eggs

sea salt and freshly ground black pepper

Preheat the oven to 210°C. Line a baking tray with baking paper.

Spread the fennel, onion and olives evenly over the prepared baking tray and drizzle over 1 tablespoon of the coconut oil. Bake for 20–30 minutes, or until the fennel is tender and beginning to turn golden. Remove the vegetables from the oven and lower the heat to 180°C.

Warm the remaining tablespoon of coconut oil in a 25 cm cast-iron frying pan over medium heat. Add the kale and garlic and sauté until the kale is soft and wilted, then stir in the roasted fennel, onion and olives.

In a bowl, whisk the eggs together with a little salt and pepper until well combined and fluffy. Pour the eggs into the pan, transfer to the oven and bake for 15 minutes, or until the frittata is set. Leave to cool slightly before cutting into wedges and digging in.

SERVES 4–6

What I love ...

Fennel is a good source of vitamin B6, which plays a vital role in breaking down carbohydrates and proteins into glucose and amino acids, which can be more easily utilised by the body for energy.

Why not make extra of this frittata and take a piece to work for lunch the next day? Leftovers are what healthy eating is all about. Maximise what you can get out of each meal and make ways to incorporate them into your life.

THE PERFECT OMELETTE with CHILLI AND ROCKET

No aspiring chef graduates from culinary school without having mastered the amazingness of the perfect cloud-like omelette, and I wanted to share with you this simple method for making yours fluffy and custardy, rather than firm or rubbery as they can sometimes be. What I love about this recipe is how simple it is – you only need one pan, it is done in moments, and it keeps you nourished and satisfied all morning. The added chilli gives it a wicked kick, while the rocket and cherry tomatoes freshen the whole plate up.

3 eggs

20 g ghee, butter or coconut oil

¼ long red chilli, finely chopped

1 handful of rocket

3 cherry tomatoes, quartered

1½ teaspoons extra-virgin olive oil

sea salt and freshly ground
black pepper

Whisk the eggs together in a bowl until light and fluffy.

Melt the ghee, butter or oil in a frying pan over high heat until runny and almost caramelised. Add the egg and, using a rubber spatula or the flat side of a fork, stir it gently, while at the same time shuffling the pan back and forth over the heat. (This keeps the eggs from sticking or browning, even while over such high heat.)

As soon as the texture of the egg changes from runny to thick and custardy, stop stirring. Scatter the chopped chilli, rocket and cherry tomatoes over the top, drizzle with the olive oil and, using a spatula, gently fold the omelette in half. Season with salt and pepper and you're good to rock and roll!

SERVES 1

Light, fluffy, this
doesn't disappoint.

ZUCCHINI FRITTERS with CREAMY CASHEW FETA

I just love fritters and make them all the time. I can't get enough of creating unique and diverse flavour combinations, and they are perfect for utilising the leftovers in my fridge. Easy to make, phenomenal to eat, zucchini fritters are definitely one of my favourites!

For the cashew feta, drain the cashew nuts and place them in a food processor or blender with the garlic, olive oil and lemon juice. Season with salt and pepper and blend until beautifully smooth, adding a dash of water if needed to loosen everything up a little. Set aside and get cracking on the fritters.

In a bowl, combine the grated zucchini, egg, almond meal, onion, garlic and chilli flakes and mix well to form a nice, thick batter.

Melt the coconut oil in a large frying pan over medium heat. Spoon the zucchini batter mixture into the pan in four loose rounds and press down lightly on each to form fritters. Cook for 2–3 minutes on each side until cooked through and golden and crunchy on the outside. Season with salt and pepper and serve with the cashew feta and your favourite mixed leaves.

SERVES 2

I don't drain the zucchini here, like many people do when making fritters, as I find the almond meal absorbs most of the water it contains. If you feel the batter is looking a little too wet, just add a little extra almond meal.

2 zucchini, grated

2 eggs, whisked

55 g (½ cup) almond meal

¼ red onion, finely diced

1 garlic clove, crushed

1 tablespoon dried chilli flakes

2 tablespoons coconut oil

sea salt and freshly ground black pepper

your favourite mixed leaves, to serve

Cashew feta (makes 230 g/ 1½ cups)

155 g (1 cup) cashew nuts, soaked in water for at least 3 hours

1 garlic clove, roughly chopped

2 tablespoons extra-virgin olive oil

juice of 1 lemon

sea salt and freshly ground black pepper

Time spent in
the kitchen is time
well spent.

CHIA and
ZUCCHINI HAZELNUT
BREAD with CASHEW
NUT BUTTER
PAGE 88

ULTIMATE DARK
CHOC-CHIP
COOKIES
PAGE 96

BAKERY

Healthy loaves, muffins,
bikkies and more

CHOCOLATE NUT
LOAF with LEMON-
MACADAMIA
BUTTER
PAGE 84

WALNUT and CINNAMON SCROLLS with COCONUT BUTTER ICING

I have such fond memories of enjoying a cinnamon scroll from the bakery at the end of my street on the way back from school. There was something so exciting about saving up my coins and devouring one as I walked home – a break between school and homework that felt delicious and comforting.

Get started by preheating the oven to 180°C and lining a baking tray with baking paper.

In a bowl, mix together the arrowroot or tapioca flour, almond meal, cinnamon, baking powder and salt until well combined. In a separate bowl, mix together the eggs, coconut oil and maple syrup. Combine the wet and dry ingredients to form a dough, then cover in plastic wrap and transfer to the fridge for 15 minutes to chill.

To make the filling, mix the ingredients together in a bowl.

Once chilled, roll out the dough between two sheets of baking paper into a 20 cm x 10 cm rectangle with a thickness of 5 mm, adding a little extra arrowroot flour if necessary to prevent it from sticking. Remove the top sheet of baking paper and sprinkle over the filling, then use the remaining sheet of baking paper to carefully roll up the dough lengthways into a cylinder.

Slice the rolled dough into eight pieces and place them, cut-side up, on the prepared baking tray. Bake the scrolls for 20 minutes or until golden brown, then set them aside on a wire rack to cool slightly.

For the coconut butter icing, mix all the ingredients together in a small bowl until well combined. Using a palette knife or spoon, smear the icing messily over the scrolls.

Go on, dig in. What are you waiting for?

MAKES 8

130 g (1 cup) arrowroot or tapioca flour, plus extra if needed

200 g (2 cups) almond meal

2 teaspoons ground cinnamon

½ teaspoon baking powder

½ teaspoon sea salt

2 eggs

80 ml (⅓ cup) coconut oil, melted

2 tablespoons maple syrup

Walnut filling

100 g (½ cup) coconut sugar

1 tablespoon ground cinnamon

2 tablespoons roughly chopped walnuts

Coconut butter icing

125 g coconut butter

3 tablespoons Vanilla Almond Milk (see page 34)

1 tablespoon maple syrup

Tip

Coconut butter is a spread made purely from ground coconut flesh, in much the same way almonds are used to make almond butter. Its creamy consistency and delicious coconut flavour make it the perfect accompaniment to these scrolls.

CHOCOLATE NUT LOAF
with LEMON—MACADAMIA BUTTER

Made predominantly from nut butter and eggs, this breakfast loaf will be unlike anything you've ever eaten before, especially when combined with the creamy, zesty goodness of the lemon–macadamia butter. I can't think of a better way to start the day.

250 g almond butter

6 eggs

80 ml (⅓ cup) maple syrup

60 g (½ cup) cacao powder

1 vanilla pod, split and seeds scraped

½ teaspoon stevia powder

½ teaspoon sea salt

½ teaspoon baking powder

2 tablespoons ground cinnamon

Lemon–macadamia butter (makes about 310 g/2 cups)

finely grated zest and juice of 1 lemon

320 g (2 cups) macadamia nuts

125 g coconut butter or coconut oil

Preheat the oven to 160°C and line a 22 cm loaf tin with baking paper.

Place the almond butter in a large mixing bowl and blitz it with a hand-held blender until nice and creamy. Add the remaining ingredients and blend together to form a nice, thick dough. Transfer the dough to the loaf tin and bake for 25 minutes or until cooked through. To test, press down gently on the top of the loaf – if it holds its shape, it's ready.

While you leave the loaf to cool, get onto the lemon–macadamia butter. Place all the ingredients in a food processor and blitz together until smooth and creamy, adding a splash or two of water if you need to loosen it up a little.

To serve, cut the loaf into slices and generously smear the lemon–macadamia butter over the top. Store the loaf and butter in separate airtight containers in the fridge for up to 5–6 days.

MAKES I LOAF

What I love ...

Almond butter is an ideal source of slow-to-digest protein, perfect for providing you with a steady source of energy during a gruelling training session. I often have a slice of this loaf as a pre-workout protein hit.

APPLE, BLUEBERRY and COCONUT MUFFINS

Apple, blueberry and coconut are definitely three of my all-time favourite flavours, and when combined into these muffins, you cannot go wrong. Quick and easy to put together, and perfect for school lunches or a weekend picnic, I don't think you need any excuse to whip up a batch of these delicious bad boys.

300 g (3 cups) almond meal

4 eggs

2 teaspoons baking powder

3 tablespoons coconut oil, melted

2 tablespoons coconut butter

1 teaspoon ground cinnamon

2 tablespoons maple syrup

1 green apple, skin on and finely diced

155 g (1 cup) blueberries

1 tablespoon shredded coconut

butter or coconut oil,
to serve (optional)

Preheat the oven to 180°C. Grease a large 6-hole or regular 12-hole muffin tin with coconut oil and line with paper cases.

In a bowl, mix together the almond meal, eggs, baking powder, coconut oil, coconut butter, cinnamon and maple syrup to form a batter. Stir through the apple and blueberries, then spoon the batter into the prepared muffin holes.

Sprinkle over the shredded coconut and bake for 35–40 minutes, or until golden on top and cooked through. Remove the muffins from the tin and allow them to cool slightly on a wire rack.

Serve warm with a nice smear of butter or coconut oil, or store in an airtight container for up to 4–5 days.

MAKES 6 LARGE OR 12 REGULAR-SIZED MUFFINS

The naturally occurring sugars found in the green apple and blueberries are a fantastic source of energy to kickstart your day, and make these muffins the perfect pre- or post-workout recovery meal or snack.

CHIA and ZUCCHINI HAZELNUT BREAD with CASHEW NUT BUTTER

This phenomenal tasting, nutrient-dense paleo bread is a staple in my house. The zucchini makes it really moist, while the chia seeds add protein and iron, making every slice of this worth its weight in gold. Making your own nut butter is relatively simple and very affordable – all you need is a powerful food processor and a few simple ingredients.

130 g (1 cup) arrowroot or tapioca flour
200 g (2 cups) hazelnut or almond meal
60 g (½ cup) chia seeds
1 teaspoon baking powder
½ teaspoon sea salt
2 tablespoons pumpkin seeds
2 tablespoons sunflower seeds
6 eggs
2 teaspoons apple cider vinegar
300 g zucchini, grated
2 tablespoons finely chopped black olives

Cashew nut butter (makes 480 g/2 cups)

470 g (3 cups) cashew nuts
1 tablespoon coconut oil, melted
pinch of sea salt

What I love ...

In spite of their size, pumpkin seeds are a nutritional powerhouse, containing a wide range of nutrients from magnesium and manganese to copper, protein and zinc.

Preheat the oven to 160°C and line a 22 cm loaf tin with baking paper.

For the cashew nut butter, place the cashew nuts in a food processor and puree on high, scraping down the sides from time to time to make sure all the nuts are blitzed, until the cashew nuts have broken down to a paste with a dough-like consistency. Add the melted coconut oil, salt and 1 tablespoon of water and continue to blend until either chunky or smooth. Everyone has their favourite style of nut butter – for chunky, just don't blend it completely so that there are still some harder bits, but for smooth, blitz until smooth and creamy. Set aside in an airtight container until needed.

Combine the arrowroot or tapioca flour, hazelnut or almond meal, chia seeds, baking powder, salt and half the pumpkin and sunflower seeds in a large bowl. In a separate bowl, whisk the eggs lightly with a fork and stir in the apple cider vinegar, grated zucchini and chopped olives. Combine the wet and dry ingredients and mix everything together using a spoon to form a thick and slightly wet dough. Pour the dough into the loaf tin and sprinkle over the remaining pumpkin and sunflower seeds.

Bake for 1 hour, or until golden on top. To test, press down gently on the top of the loaf – if it holds its shape, it's ready. Enjoy fresh out of the oven spread with the cashew nut butter or, if eating later, toast under the grill. To store, cover in plastic wrap or keep in an airtight container for up to 5 days.

MAKES 1 LOAF

See a pic of me on page 90

This nut butter recipe works equally well with any type of nut you like and tastes fantastic with your breakfast, on your desserts and in your smoothies. I store my homemade nut butter in an airtight container in the fridge, and allow it to soften slightly at room temperature for best results. It will keep for up to 2 weeks.

COCONUT BREAKFAST LOAF with RASPBERRY–CHIA JAM

This little baby is all about replicating a breakfast staple we have come to know and love … and for me it's definitely the next best thing to sliced bread! Serve it with eggs and bacon or, better still, with a smear of my incredible raspberry–chia jam. The chia seeds act as a binding agent, making it spread beautifully.

Preheat the oven to 180°C and line a 22 cm loaf tin with baking paper.

Place the coconut flour, coconut oil, LSA, baking powder, salt, egg and honey in a bowl and mix together well with a hand-held blender to form a smooth dough. Transfer the dough to the loaf tin and bake for 35–40 minutes, or until golden on top. To test, press down gently on the top of the loaf – if it holds its shape, it's ready.

While the loaf is cooking, get cracking on the jam by placing the raspberries, maple syrup and vanilla seeds in a food processor or blender and blitzing together until smooth. Tip the mixture into a bowl, stir in the chia seeds and transfer to the fridge for at least 10 minutes to set, then enjoy spread over your freshly baked loaf.

MAKES 1 LOAF

See a pic of me on page 91

270 g (2 cups) coconut flour
250 ml (1 cup) coconut oil, melted
25 g (¼ cup) LSA (linseed, sunflower seed and almond mix)
1 teaspoon baking powder
1 teaspoon sea salt
8 eggs, beaten
2 tablespoons honey

**Raspberry–chia jam
(makes about 160 g/1 cup)**

250 g (2 cups) raspberries, fresh
1 tablespoon maple syrup
1 vanilla pod, split and scraped
3 tablespoons chia seeds

The jam will keep in the fridge for up to 5 days. I like to keep the loaf in an airtight container in the fridge, where it will last for up to 6 days – grill it for best results.

CHIA and
ZUCCHINI HAZELNUT
BREAD with CASHEW
NUT BUTTER
PAGE 88

COCONUT BREAKFAST LOAF with RASPBERRY—CHIA JAM PAGE 89

ONE BOWL CHOC-NUT RASPBERRY BROWNIES

Chocolate and raspberry has got to be one of my favourite flavour combinations. Here the bitterness of the cacao powder together with the tartness of the raspberries goes off like a party in your mouth.

Preheat the oven to 180°C and line a 20 cm square baking tin with baking paper.

Place all the ingredients except the raspberries in a bowl and mix to form a batter.

Spread the batter evenly over the prepared baking tin, dot the raspberries evenly over the surface and bake for 25–30 minutes, or until the top is looking firm and crunchy and gives a little resistance when lightly touched. Remove from the oven and leave to cool in the tin, then cut into 12 pieces. Store in an airtight container for up to 7 days.

MAKES 12

60 g (½ cup) cacao powder
100 ml coconut oil, melted
125 g Lemon–Macadamia Butter (see page 84)
140 g (1 cup) coconut sugar
4 eggs
100 g (1 cup) almond meal
160 g (1 cup) macadamia nuts, roughly chopped
½ teaspoon ground cinnamon
1 vanilla pod, split and scraped
pinch of sea salt
125 g (1 cup) fresh raspberries

What I love ...

Macadamia nuts contain more heart-healthy monounsaturated fat per serving than any other nut. This 'good' fat helps lower unhealthy cholesterol levels and high blood pressure.

MOVE and PLAY

I want to create a new way of thinking about exercise, based on being active by simply moving your body and playing. You see, some people view exercise as something that has to be rigidly structured and performed in a gym or group fitness class or the like, when in fact the best way to be the healthiest and happiest version of yourself is to simply move your body and play in life!

First and foremost, moving your body should be something you enjoy … because ultimately you're the one doing it, remember! Make sure that whatever you choose to do is suitable for your age, fitness level and health condition. This will therefore mean something different for everybody. It doesn't have to require equipment or a gym membership, and it is often better when it involves the great outdoors. I love making the most of my natural surroundings, whether national park or wide, open beaches. Fantastic examples are taking the dog for a run, getting out into the ocean for a swim, or simply going for a beautiful long walk with a friend. Whatever movement you enjoy, make it a part of your everyday routine. Cut down on 'screen' time (be that TV or the multitude of tech devices that are now part of our day-to-day lives) and get amongst the amazing real world out there.

The key is to make movement as fun as possible, and this is where the 'play' comes into it. I like to think of it as the combination of moving and having fun. It could be kicking the footy in the park with the kids, friends or family, or playing fetch with the dog. Whatever it is that puts a smile on your face, do that more often – because happiness and being active go hand in hand, and when we align doing that with clean nutrition, we truly reach new heights.

ULTIMATE DARK CHOC-CHIP COOKIES

I know it's a pretty big call to make, but these choc-chip cookies *are* the ultimate! What sets them apart is the fact that the dark chocolate chips are made from scratch too, making them cleaner, tastier and more decadent than ever before. Make a big batch and time how long they last.

200 g (2 cups) almond meal

1 teaspoon baking powder

1 teaspoon ground cinnamon

pinch of sea salt

125 ml (½ cup) coconut oil, melted, plus extra if needed

1 egg yolk

2 tablespoons honey or maple syrup

1 vanilla pod, split and scraped

Raw chocolate (makes 250 g/2 cups)

100 g (1 cup) cacao butter

100 g (1 cup) cacao powder

3 tablespoons maple syrup

1 vanilla pod, split and scraped

Line two baking trays with baking paper.

For the raw chocolate, stir together all the ingredients in a saucepan over low heat until lovely and runny. Pour the melted chocolate mixture over one of the prepared baking trays and let it set in the freezer until rock solid.

Once solid, break the chocolate into small chips using a rolling pin or the end of a wooden spoon, then return to the freezer until needed.

Preheat the oven to 180°C.

In a bowl, combine the almond meal, baking powder, cinnamon and salt and mix well. Now stir in the coconut oil, egg yolk, honey or maple syrup and vanilla seeds to bring everything together to form a dough, adding a little extra coconut oil if needed to make the batter stick together a little better. Gently stir in 100 g of the chocolate chips.

Arrange tablespoonfuls of the mixture on the second baking tray 3 cm apart and bake for 8–10 minutes, or until golden brown. Remove from the oven and leave to cool and firm on the tray for 5–10 minutes before eating.

MAKES ABOUT 10

Any leftover chocolate chips are great added to smoothies, sprinkled on top of desserts, or simply enjoyed as a little snack in their own right.

The BEST BANANA and RASPBERRY BREAD with SPICED CARAMEL SAUCE

I don't know many people who don't love banana bread. It's so incredibly easy to make, plus it's the perfect way to make use of overripe bananas. Is it bad that I sometimes deliberately let my bananas go brown so I have an excuse to make this little number? I hope you love it, guys!

4 eggs

80 ml (⅓ cup) coconut oil, melted

200 g (2 cups) almond meal

2 tablespoons coconut butter

2 very ripe bananas, mashed, and 1 extra banana, sliced in half lengthways

2 tablespoons chia seeds

2 tablespoons desiccated coconut

60 g (½ cup) walnuts, toasted and crushed

1 teaspoon ground cinnamon

125 g (1 cup) fresh raspberries

Spiced caramel sauce (makes about 1 cup)

250 ml (1 cup) coconut cream

125 ml (½ cup) maple syrup

40 g unsalted butter or ghee

1 teaspoon ground cinnamon

½ teaspoon ground nutmeg

1 vanilla pod, split and scraped

pinch of sea salt

Preheat the oven to 180°C and line a 22 cm loaf tin with baking paper.

In a large bowl, mix together the eggs, coconut oil, almond meal, coconut butter, mashed banana, chia seeds, coconut, walnuts and cinnamon to form a nice thick batter, then gently stir in the raspberries (you want them to stay as whole and luscious as possible, so try not to break them up too much).

Pour the batter into the loaf tin and place the sliced banana halves on top, cut-side up. Bake for 30 minutes, or until the loaf is golden and the banana slices are beautifully caramelised. Leave to cool in the tin.

Meanwhile, make the spiced caramel sauce by whisking together all the ingredients in a saucepan over medium heat. Bring to the boil, then reduce to a simmer and cook over medium–high heat, stirring often, for 30 minutes, or until nice and thick (be careful to keep stirring to prevent the mixture from burning on the bottom of the pan). Once ready, remove from the heat and allow to cool slightly before enjoying with the banana bread.

MAKES 1 LOAF

Transfer any leftover caramel sauce to an airtight container and keep refrigerated until needed, gently warming it in a pan over low heat whenever you wish to enjoy it. The sauce will keep for up to 2 weeks in the fridge.

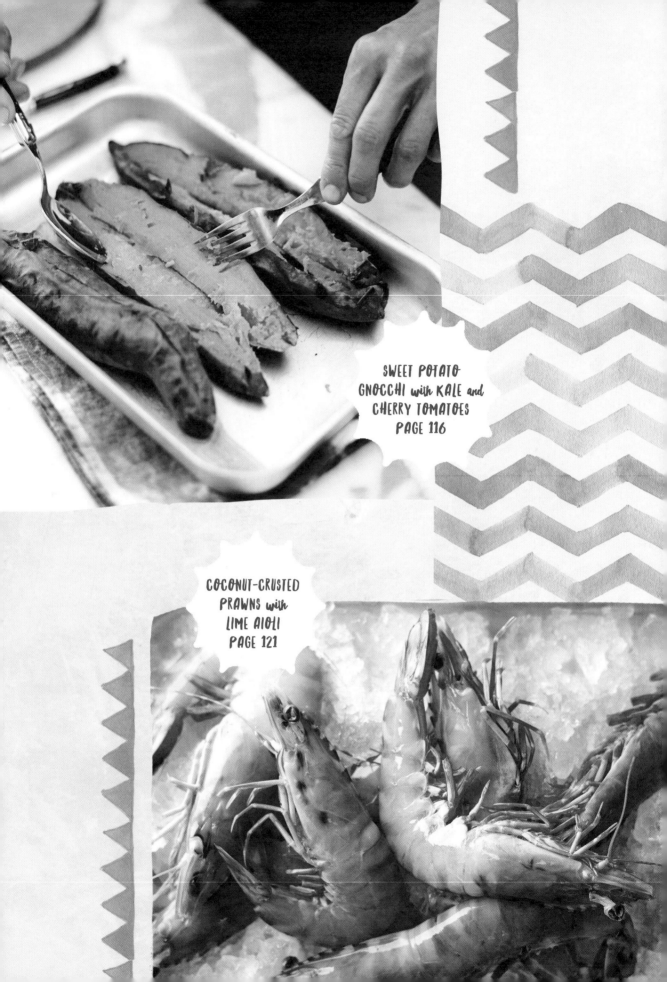

SWEET POTATO
GNOCCHI with KALE and
CHERRY TOMATOES
PAGE 116

COCONUT-CRUSTED
PRAWNS with
LIME AIOLI
PAGE 121

MAINS

*Fuss-free feasts for
every occasion*

Take a culinary
holiday and taste the
flavours of the world.

OVEN-BAKED
RIBS with SPICY
BARBECUE SAUCE
PAGE 140

RAW VEGETABLE SALAD with MACADAMIA PESTO

Crunchy and textured, the flavours just burst out of this incredible raw salad. It's so quick and simple to prepare, and the combination of the zingy ginger dressing with the chunky macadamia pesto is a match made in clean-living heaven.

For the macadamia pesto, simply pulse all the ingredients together in a food processor until well combined. I personally like mine nice and chunky, so I don't go too far with the blending action. Set aside.

Place the beetroot, zucchini, carrot, capsicum, cabbage and onion in a large bowl. Mix together well and set aside.

In a separate bowl, whisk together all of the dressing ingredients until well combined. Season with a little salt and pepper, pour over the prepared vegetables and toss everything together so that the vegetables are well coated in the dressing.

Pile the dressed vegetables onto a platter and top with the toasted macadamia nuts, chia seeds and dollops of macadamia pesto. Serve with lemon cheeks and cauliflower couscous.

SERVES 4

This vibrant, green macadamia pesto is great for dressing all your salads, serving as a side with meats or even topping your paleo pizzas! Stored in an airtight container, it will keep in the fridge for up to 5 days.

2 beetroot, peeled and cut into matchsticks

2 zucchini, cut into matchsticks

2 carrots, cut into matchsticks

1 green capsicum, deseeded and cut into matchsticks

¼ red cabbage, finely sliced

½ red onion, finely sliced

45 g (about 15) crushed toasted macadamia nuts

2 tablespoons black chia seeds

lemon cheeks, to serve

100 g (1 cup) Cauliflower Couscous (see Tip page 167), to serve

Macadamia pesto

1 large bunch of basil, leaves picked

1 large bunch of flat-leaf parsley, leaves picked

2 garlic cloves

finely grated zest and juice of 2 lemons

90 g macadamia nuts

125 ml (½ cup) extra-virgin olive oil

pinch of sea salt

Dressing

2.5 cm piece of ginger, peeled and finely grated

3 tablespoons avocado oil

2 tablespoons apple cider vinegar

juice of 2 lemons

½ long red chilli, finely chopped

2 tablespoons finely chopped coriander leaves

sea salt and freshly ground black pepper

MIDDLE EASTERN WHOLE ROASTED CAULIFLOWER

I have a really strong affinity for Middle Eastern food. It has a beautiful simplicity in its preparation and construction, yet the flavours are rich and bold. So here it is, my Middle Eastern-inspired whole roasted cauliflower. Enjoy, legends.

1 large head of cauliflower

3 tablespoons coconut oil, melted

1 teaspoon sea salt

2 teaspoons ground cumin

2 teaspoons sweet paprika

2 teaspoons ground coriander

135 g (½ cup) tahini, plus extra for drizzling

1 handful of flat-leaf parsley leaves, finely chopped

a squeeze of lemon juice

lightly toasted pine nuts, to serve

Get started by preheating the oven to 170°C and lining a large baking tray with baking paper.

Trim off the outer cauliflower leaves and cut away the bottom of the stalk so the cauliflower can sit flat, then cut a cross into the base of the trimmed stalk.

Using your hands, rub the whole cauliflower liberally with the coconut oil and then sprinkle all over with the salt, cumin, paprika and coriander. Bake for 2 hours, or until tender (you can check the cauliflower by piercing it with a paring knife – if it goes through easily, it's cooked).

Spread the tahini evenly over the base of a serving dish. Sit the roasted cauliflower on top, sprinkle over the parsley and squeeze over the lemon juice. Drizzle over a little extra tahini and sprinkle with pine nuts to serve. I don't think anyone at the table is going to be disappointed.

SERVES 4

See a pic of me on page 108

What I love ...

Cauliflower is a rich source of vitamin C, so put those oranges back in the fruit bowl and get roasting this bad boy!

CRUNCHY APPLE
and FENNEL SALAD with
ROASTED BEETROOT
PAGE 113

MIDDLE EASTERN
WHOLE ROASTED
CAULIFLOWER
PAGE 106

RAW
PAD THAI
PAGE 110

RAW PAD THAI

People often think I eat a lot of meat with every meal, when in fact it's only a moderate amount compared with the many amazing and nourishing vegetables I consume throughout my day. This raw pad Thai is a great example of how you can increase your daily veggie intake while not compromising on flavour. It is said that vegetables in their raw state retain more of their nutrients, which sounds pretty good to me!

2 zucchini

2 carrots

4 yellow squash

1 red capsicum, deseeded and cut into matchsticks

1 yellow capsicum, deseeded and cut into matchsticks

1 green capsicum, deseeded and cut into matchsticks

2 spring onions, finely sliced

2 long red chillies, deseeded and chopped

1 bunch of coriander, leaves picked and chopped

3 tablespoons sesame seeds

2 tablespoons crushed toasted hazelnuts

Dressing

125 ml (½ cup) canned coconut milk

3 tablespoons tahini

finely grated zest and juice of 2 limes

1 tablespoon coconut aminos (see Tip on page 140)

2 tablespoons avocado oil

1 tablespoon sugar-free fish sauce

pinch of sea salt

Using a mandoline, spiraliser or very sharp knife, cut the zucchini, carrot and squash into fine vegetable noodles. Place these in a large bowl and add the capsicum, spring onion, chilli and coriander.

For the dressing, put all the ingredients in a separate bowl and whisk together until well combined.

Pile the salad onto a massive serving platter, drizzle over the dressing and top with the sesame seeds and toasted hazelnuts.

SERVES 4

To bump up the protein in this incredible pad Thai, simply add some cold, shredded, poached chicken.

CRUNCHY APPLE and FENNEL SALAD with ROASTED BEETROOT

This great little salad is perfect for pulling out when entertaining. I simply love the combination of the earthy beetroot, sweet apple and bitter fennel – there's something for everyone – and you can't go wrong with the added crunch of toasted walnuts and sunflower seeds.

Get started by preheating the oven to 200°C and lining two baking trays with baking paper.

Spread out the roughly chopped kale on one of the prepared trays in a single layer, massage the leaves with the coconut oil and season with salt. Bake until the leaves turn crispy – you'll be looking at 10–15 minutes.

Meanwhile, place the beetroot on the other baking tray with the garlic and fennel seeds. Drizzle over the avocado oil and mix everything together well. Cover with foil and bake for 20 minutes. Remove the foil and bake for a further 20 minutes, or until the beetroot is beautiful and tender. Set aside to cool completely.

To assemble, place the fennel, apple, parsley and coriander in a bowl and mix together really well. Toss with the extra-virgin olive oil, apple cider vinegar and lemon juice, then pile onto a large serving platter. Top with the roasted beetroot mixture, scatter over the kale chips, sunflower seeds and walnuts and garnish with a few of the reserved fennel fronds. Season with salt and pepper and dig in!

SERVES 4

175 g kale, stalks removed and leaves roughly chopped
2 tablespoons coconut oil, melted
sea salt and freshly ground black pepper
2 large beetroot, peeled and quartered
6 garlic cloves, roughly chopped
1 tablespoon fennel seeds
2 tablespoons avocado oil
2 fennel bulbs, thinly sliced and fronds reserved
2 red apples, cored and finely sliced
1 bunch of flat-leaf parsley, leaves picked and roughly chopped
1 bunch of coriander, leaves picked and roughly chopped
3 tablespoons extra-virgin olive oil
2 tablespoons apple cider vinegar
juice of 1 lemon
3 tablespoons sunflower seeds, toasted
3 tablespoons crushed toasted walnuts

What I love ...

Fennel is famous for its stomach-calming benefits, making it very popular for those wanting to alleviate any digestive issues.

Tips

Not a fan of the raw fennel in this salad? Try roasting it in a hot oven with coconut oil, cherry tomatoes and olives until it becomes beautiful and caramelised. Alternatively, to get the fantastic health benefits of fennel, try incorporating fennel seeds into your tea.

OVEN-BAKED EGGPLANT with TZATZIKI and POMEGRANATE

I have always been a massive fan of Greek food as it's full of interesting flavours but has a simplicity that makes it really achievable for home cooks. I wanted to share with you a favourite Greek dish of mine with a paleo spin – perfect for serving on a large share platter in the middle of the table.

4 large eggplants

80 ml (⅓ cup) coconut oil, melted

sea salt

8 thyme sprigs

Paleo tzatziki

4 Lebanese cucumbers, peeled and chopped

1 garlic clove, grated

1 ripe avocado

juice of 1 lemon

2 tablespoons extra-virgin olive oil

2 tablespoons finely chopped dill

2 tablespoons finely chopped chives

1 small handful of mint leaves, roughly chopped

sea salt and freshly ground black pepper

To serve

pomegranate seeds

mint leaves

lemon wedges

Preheat the oven to 200°C. Line a baking tray with baking paper.

Slice the eggplants in half lengthways and score the flesh deeply in a diamond crosshatch pattern. Generously rub the eggplant halves with the coconut oil and season with salt. Arrange each eggplant half, cut-side down, on the baking tray on top of a sprig or two of thyme. Transfer to the oven and roast for 40 minutes, or until the eggplant flesh is soft and the skins are a caramel colour.

Meanwhile, make the tzatziki topping. Put the cucumber and garlic in a food processor with the avocado, lemon juice and olive oil and pulse until you get a nice thick, creamy texture. Tip this mixture into a bowl, stir in the chopped herbs and season with salt and pepper to taste.

Arrange the eggplant halves, cut-side up, on a serving platter and top with a generous smattering of the tzatziki. Garnish with a few pomegranate seeds and mint leaves, and serve with some lemon wedges.

SERVES 4

This tzatziki makes an incredible dip for seed crackers or paleo toast. Alternatively, try tossing it through cauliflower couscous (see Tip page 167) or salads for extra zing. These eggplants can be refrigerated and enjoyed cold the next day with meats and salads.

SWEET POTATO GNOCCHI with KALE and CHERRY TOMATOES

Since transitioning to a primarily paleo lifetsyle, I haven't had the opportunity to indulge in traditional pasta-based meals. I love gnocchi and am so excited to share with you this clean-living version packed full of flavour and vibrancy.

800 g (about 2 large) sweet potatoes

300 g (2 cups) quinoa flour, plus extra for dusting

sea salt and freshly ground black pepper

1 egg yolk

40 g butter

2 tablespoons coconut oil

1 garlic clove, finely diced

1 long red chilli, deseeded and finely diced

200 g cherry tomatoes, halved

100 g baby kale leaves

finely grated zest and juice of 1 lemon

Get started by preheating the oven to 180°C and lining two baking trays with baking paper.

Arrange the sweet potatoes on one of the prepared trays and roast for 1 hour until they are lovely and soft and the skin starts to crisp. Cut them open, scoop the flesh into a bowl and mash it with a potato masher or fork until smooth. Stir in the quinoa flour and season with salt and pepper, then add the egg yolk and gently mix everything together to a dough-like consistency, adding a little water if the mixture is too dry or a little extra quinoa flour if it's looking too wet.

Turn the dough mixture out onto a floured work surface and divide into four equal-sized pieces. Roll these pieces into long logs about 5 cm in thickness and cut into 5 cm lengths. Press each cut piece gently with a fork to create indentations.

Bring a large saucepan of salted water to the boil, add the gnocchi in batches and cook for 1–2 minutes, or until the gnocchi float to the surface. Remove with a slotted spoon and set aside on the other lined baking tray. Once you've boiled them all, melt the butter in a large frying pan and fry the gnocchi in batches until crisp and golden. Set them aside and keep warm while you crack on with the topping.

Melt the coconut oil in a large frying pan over medium–high heat, add the garlic and chilli and fry for 2–3 minutes until softened and caramelised. Add the cherry tomatoes, stir to coat with the chilli and garlic and cook for a further 2 minutes until softened, then stir in the baby kale leaves and cook until slightly wilted. Remove from the heat and drizzle with lemon juice.

Divide the gnocchi among four plates, spoon over the kale and cherry tomato topping and sprinkle with the lemon zest.

SERVES 4

Nothing beats the taste
of homemade pasta.

Take your time and
enjoy the process. ↗

I'm sure this is what the
Italians do, yeah? ⤳

↑

Creating something
from scratch is
massively rewarding.

COCONUT-CRUSTED PRAWNS with LIME AIOLI

It doesn't get much better than crispy fried coconut prawns. Crunchy on the outside and tender in the middle, this summer favourite is a definite crowd-pleaser. It's also paleo approved, which is awesome to know!

To make the aioli, place the egg yolks, mustard, apple cider vinegar, lime juice, garlic and a pinch of salt in a bowl and whiz together with a hand-held blender. Continuing to blend, slowly add the extra-virgin olive oil in a thin, even stream until all the oil has been added and the aioli is thick and creamy. Season with salt and pepper, cover with plastic wrap and keep refrigerated until needed.

Place the beaten egg in a bowl. Combine the arrowroot or tapioca flour, shredded coconut, coconut flour, salt, paprika and chilli powder (if using) in a second bowl. Dip the butterflied prawns first into the egg wash, letting any excess fall off into the bowl, then coat really well in the coconut mixture.

Over medium heat, melt enough coconut oil to fill a heavy-based saucepan or wok to a depth of 5 cm. Heat the oil to 180°C. To test if it is hot enough, simply drop a small piece of batter into the oil – if it sizzles and bubbles, you're good to go. Add the prawns to the hot oil in batches (you don't want to overcrowd the pan with this one) and cook for 4–5 minutes, or until golden brown on the outside and just cooked through. Once cooked, transfer the prawns to a plate lined with paper towel to drain off any excess oil. Keep warm while you cook the remaining prawns.

Serve the prawns on a large platter with a big bowl of the lime aioli for dipping and some lime cheeks for squeezing over the top.

SERVES 4

2 eggs, beaten
2 tablespoons arrowroot or tapioca flour
120 g (2 cups) shredded coconut
3 tablespoons coconut flour
1 teaspoon sea salt
1 teaspoon sweet paprika
1 teaspoon chilli powder (optional)
800 g raw banana prawns, peeled, deveined and butterflied
coconut oil, for frying
lime cheeks, to serve

Lime aioli (makes 500 ml/2 cups)

4 egg yolks
2 teaspoons dijon mustard
2 tablespoons apple cider vinegar
juice of 1 lime
3 garlic cloves, finely chopped
sea salt and freshly ground black pepper
400 ml extra-virgin olive oil

Take the lime aioli to the next level by adding a little bit of heat – finely chop a small bird's eye chilli and stir it through the prepared aioli for an extra hit. You can store leftover aioli in the fridge for up to 7 days in an airtight container.

SALT and PEPPER SQUID with CHARGRILLED ZUCCHINI

I am a massive fan of squid – it's fresh, light and high in protein. I particularly love it like this, slightly crispy on the outside with a tastebud-zinging coating of salt and pepper. I've paired this with vibrant chargrilled zucchini to add a little colour to the plate. Get stuck in!

30 g (¼ cup) arrowroot or tapioca flour

2 teaspoons ground white pepper

2 teaspoons sea salt

2 teaspoons garlic powder

600 g squid hoods, cleaned, scored and cut into 10 cm x 6 cm strips

3 tablespoons coconut oil

2 long red chillies, finely sliced

a squeeze of lemon juice

1 small bunch of flat-leaf parsley, leaves picked and roughly chopped

3 tablespoons crushed toasted cashew nuts

lime cheeks, to serve

Chargrilled zucchini

4 zucchini (2 green, 2 yellow), sliced lengthways into thin strips

2 tablespoons coconut oil, melted

Combine the arrowroot or tapioca flour, white pepper, salt and garlic powder in a large bowl. Add the squid pieces and toss to coat.

Melt the coconut oil in a deep frying pan or wok over medium–high heat. Add the fresh chilli and stir-fry for 30 seconds or so until slightly softened. Add the squid and stir-fry for 1–2 minutes, or until the squid is crispy, lightly golden and just cooked through. Set aside.

For the chargrilled zucchini, brush the zucchini strips with the melted coconut oil, transfer to a hot chargrill pan or barbecue and cook for 2–3 minutes on each side until tender, soft and nicely charred.

Arrange the chargrilled zucchini pieces on a large platter and top with the crispy salt and pepper squid. Squeeze over a little lemon juice, sprinkle with flat-leaf parsley and scatter over the cashew nuts. Serve with lime cheeks.

SERVES 4

Try serving this with my epic Lime Aioli (page 121).

GRILLED GINGER OCEAN TROUT with SAUTÉED KALE

This is one of those perfect recipes for the typical weeknight meal. It doesn't require too much prep and can be whipped up without hassle to wind down after a big day. I've used a whole piece of ocean trout instead of fillets for this photo, so depending on how many people you're serving, or the occasion, you can mix it up.

4 x 150–180 g ocean trout fillets, skin on

2 tablespoons coconut oil, melted

2 long red chillies, deseeded and cut into matchsticks

2 garlic cloves, finely diced

3 tablespoons coconut aminos (see Tip page 140)

2.5 cm piece of ginger, peeled and grated

175 g kale, stalks removed

finely grated zest and juice of 1 lemon

2 tablespoons sesame seeds

2 tablespoons crushed toasted hazelnuts

Preheat the grill to medium. Line a baking tray with baking paper.

Place the ocean trout fillets, skin-side down, on the prepared baking tray and rub with 1 tablespoon of the coconut oil.

In a bowl, combine the chilli, garlic, coconut aminos and ginger. Drizzle the mixture over the trout fillets and grill for about 10–12 minutes, turning over halfway through cooking, until the fish is cooked through and the skin is nice and crispy.

While the fish is cooking, sauté the kale in a frying pan with the remaining coconut oil over medium heat for 2–3 minutes, or until softened. Remove from the heat, add the lemon zest and juice and mix together well.

Divide the fish fillets and kale among serving plates and top with the sesame seeds and toasted hazelnuts.

SERVES 4

ORANGE and HAZELNUT-CRUSTED SALMON FILLETS with CHERRY TOMATO, FENNEL and OLIVE SALAD

In the warmer summer months, many of my meals are a combination of fresh seafood and zesty salads. Seafood and citrus are just the perfect combination, and I think you'll love the flavours that burst out of this simple and delicious dish.

Get started by preheating the oven to 200°C and lining two baking trays with baking paper.

Using a mortar and pestle, pound the hazelnuts together with 1 tablespoon of the coconut oil and the orange zest and juice to form a lovely, smooth paste. Set aside.

Arrange the salmon fillets on one of the prepared trays and bake for 5 minutes. Turn the fillets over, top with the hazelnut mixture and cook for a further 5 minutes, or until the fish is cooked through and the hazelnut crust is golden brown. Set aside to rest.

Meanwhile, place the sliced fennel, cherry tomatoes and olives on the other baking tray, drizzle with the remaining tablespoon of coconut oil and season well with salt and pepper. Roast for 15–20 minutes, or until the fennel is beautifully golden and starting to shrivel. Remove from the oven and leave to cool slightly, then tip into a bowl and mix together with your choice of salad greens and the orange segments.

Divide the salmon fillets and salad among four plates, scatter over a few extra toasted hazelnuts and serve.

SERVES 4

100 g (¾ cup) toasted hazelnuts, plus extra to serve
2 tablespoons coconut oil, melted
2 oranges, 1 juiced and zested, 1 peeled and segmented
4 x 150–180 g salmon fillets, skin removed
1 large fennel bulb, thinly sliced
200 g cherry tomatoes
50 g black olives, pitted and halved
sea salt and freshly ground black pepper
3 large handfuls of rocket, watercress or micro herbs

What I love ...

Hazelnuts are packed full of dietary fibre, making them a fantastic choice for those wanting to keep regular, if you know what I mean.

SEARED TUNA STEAKS with RADISH, CUCUMBER and DILL SALAD

If there's one ingredient I should use more often in the kitchen it's radishes! They look so pretty on the plate, are high in vitamin C and potassium and make the perfect cold and crisp accompaniment to grilled fish or chicken. Here I have paired them with the freshness of cucumber and the meatiness of sashimi-grade tuna, which should be served quite rare to enjoy it at its best.

1–2 tablespoons coconut oil

4 x 150–200 g sashimi-grade tuna steaks

Radish, cucumber and dill salad

4 Lebanese cucumbers, finely sliced into discs

150 g radishes, finely sliced into discs

finely grated zest and juice of 1 lemon

1 tablespoon maple syrup

1 bunch of chives, finely chopped

1 bunch of dill, finely chopped

2 tablespoons toasted sunflower seeds

sea salt and freshly ground black pepper

Place the veggie slices in a bowl with the remaining salad ingredients and toss together well. Season with salt and pepper to taste and set aside.

Melt the coconut oil in a heavy-based frying pan over high heat, add the tuna steaks and sear for between 30 seconds and no more than 1 minute on each side. All you are looking for here is a little colour and a caramelised outside; the tuna should still be beautifully pink on the inside.

Serve the tuna steaks with the radish, cucumber and dill salad.

SERVES 4

What I love ...

Packed full of healthy omega-3 fatty acids, tuna is a fantastic clean source of protein that has been proven to have anti-inflammatory health benefits.

Tip

I like to trim the tuna steaks to make them all the same size and present beautifully!

SAN CHOY BOW

When I was a child, the local Chinese restaurant was my family's go-to for special occasions. On many an evening after a family function or school ceremony we would find ourselves feeding our faces while spinning the lazy Susan around and around, getting our helpings of all that was on offer. One of my favourite dishes was the entree of san choy bow. Already a pretty clean dish, here's my clean-living version.

1 tablespoon coconut oil

2 garlic cloves, grated

1 onion, finely diced

2 teaspoons grated ginger

600 g chicken mince

1 teaspoon chilli powder

1 carrot, grated

2 tablespoons coconut aminos
(see Tip page 140)

1 tablespoon sugar-free fish sauce,
plus extra to serve

1 tablespoon maple syrup

2 long red chillies, deseeded
and chopped

4 spring onions, finely chopped

8 large iceberg lettuce leaves

To serve

bean sprouts

fresh coriander leaves,
roughly chopped

toasted and crushed cashew nuts

lime wedges

Melt the coconut oil in a large frying pan or wok over medium heat. Add the garlic, onion and ginger and stir-fry for a couple of minutes until nice and caramelised. Chuck in the chicken mince, chilli powder and grated carrot and stir-fry for a further 4 minutes, or until the chicken is cooked through and the carrot is softened. Add the coconut aminos, fish sauce, maple syrup, chopped chilli and spring onions and stir-fry for another 2 minutes, then remove from the heat and get ready to lettuce up!

Arrange the lettuce leaves on a serving plate. Spoon a generous helping of the chicken mixture into each of your lettuce 'cups' and top with some bean sprouts, coriander leaves, toasted cashew nuts and a squeeze of fresh lime juice.

SERVES 4

TEXAS ROAST CHICKEN with CREAMY WHITE COLESLAW and SWEET POTATO CHIPS

I want to bring you the real flavours of Texas with this incredible tasting, easy-to-cook roast chicken. Everyone loves a good roast, and when combined with these flavour combinations you simply cannot go wrong.

Get started by preheating the oven to 220°C and lightly greasing a roasting tin with coconut oil.

In a small bowl, mix the salt, paprika, maple syrup, chilli powder, garlic powder, cayenne and cumin with the coconut oil to create a delicious paste. Rub this all over the chicken, being sure to get into all the little tight spots.

Pierce one of the lemons several times with a sharp knife and stuff it inside the bird's cavity. Squeeze the other lemon all over the chicken, then place the bird in the prepared roasting tin. Roast for 1 hour to 1 hour 20 minutes, or until the juices run clear when a chicken thigh is pierced with a skewer.

While the chicken is cooking, make the slaw and chips. For the slaw, combine the cabbage and carrot in a bowl, stir in the remaining ingredients and mix everything together well. Transfer to the refrigerator and leave to cool for 1 hour.

For the chips, place the sweet potato pieces on a large baking tray lined with baking paper. Drizzle with the coconut oil, season with a generous amount of salt and pepper and transfer to the oven with the chicken. Bake for 35–45 minutes, turning regularly, until golden and crunchy.

Once the chicken is cooked, remove it from the oven and cover it with foil. Leave it to rest for 20 minutes before carving it up and serving with the slaw and chips.

SERVES 4

For an extra boost of flavour, try serving this dish with my wonderful Chimichurri (see page 71).

2 teaspoons sea salt
2 teaspoons sweet paprika
2 teaspoons maple syrup
1 tablespoon chilli powder
1 teaspoon garlic powder
1 teaspoon cayenne pepper
1 teaspoon ground cumin
2 tablespoons coconut oil, melted
1 x 1.5 kg whole chicken
2 lemons

Coleslaw

½ green cabbage, outer leaves removed, very finely sliced
1 large carrot, finely sliced
½ cup Lime Aioli (see page 121) (optional)
1–2 tablespoons wholegrain mustard
1 teaspoon sweet paprika
1 teaspoon sea salt
juice of 1 lemon
3 tablespoons apple cider vinegar
1 handful of coriander leaves, roughly chopped

Sweet potato chips

2 large sweet potatoes, skin on, cut into 5 cm x 3 cm pieces
80 ml (⅓ cup) coconut oil, melted
sea salt and freshly ground black pepper

SPICY PORK BURGERS with MEXICAN RED CABBAGE SLAW

Breakfast, lunch or dinner, these burgers are one of my go-to meals whenever I need a feed. They can pretty much be paired with anything, and if you don't feel like pork you can always use beef, turkey, chicken or lamb! Get creative and play around with the flavour combinations and you'll soon be enjoying these as much as I do.

600 g pork mince

1 bunch of coriander, leaves picked and finely chopped

1 teaspoon ground cumin

½ teaspoon ground coriander

1 teaspoon sweet paprika

1 teaspoon cayenne pepper

1 long red chilli, finely diced

2 garlic cloves, grated

2 tablespoons almond meal

1 egg

sea salt and freshly ground black pepper

1–2 tablespoons coconut oil

Red cabbage slaw

½ red cabbage, outer leaves removed, finely shredded

1 red apple, cored and sliced into very thin discs

1 bunch of coriander, leaves picked and chopped

3 tablespoons pumpkin seeds

1 teaspoon sweet paprika

3 tablespoons apple cider vinegar

3 tablespoons avocado oil

finely grated zest and juice of 2 limes

juice of 1 lemon

1 tablespoon maple syrup

Get started by making the cabbage slaw. In a large bowl, combine the cabbage and apple, then stir in the coriander and pumpkin seeds and mix well. In a separate bowl, whisk together the paprika, vinegar, avocado oil, lime zest and juice, lemon juice and maple syrup to make a dressing. Pour this over the slaw and toss well to coat. The reason we make this first is because the longer you let the cabbage sit in the dressing, the more it will soften, which is a really nice result. Place the prepared slaw in the fridge and get cracking on the burgers.

Place the pork mince, coriander, spices, chilli, garlic, almond meal and egg in a large bowl. Using your hands, mix everything together really well so that the flavourings are evenly distributed through the mince. Season the mixture well with salt and pepper, then divide it into four evenly sized patties.

Melt the coconut oil in a large frying pan over medium heat, add the patties and fry for about 4–5 minutes on each side, until nicely golden and cooked through. Serve alongside the delicious cabbage slaw.

SERVES 4

What I love ...

Red cabbage is an amazing source of vitamin C, which has been proven to help maintain beautiful skin and delay the ageing process.

This burger won't leave you missing the bun! Stack your salad high.

OVEN-BAKED RIBS with SPICY BARBECUE SAUCE

I wanted to give you guys a recipe that highlights the deliciousness of pork ribs – a really affordable cut of meat that's packed full of flavour. Now, not all of you may be keen to get cooking on the barbecue, which is why I have made these ribs oven-baked and suitable for everyone. When paired with my spicy paleo barbecue sauce, you'll be fighting people off for the last rib!

2 kg pork ribs

2 tablespoons sweet paprika

2 tablespoons garlic powder

2 tablespoons onion powder

2 tablespoons hot chilli powder

2 tablespoons cayenne pepper

2 tablespoons ground cumin

2 teaspoons freshly ground black pepper

2 teaspoons sea salt

80 ml (⅓ cup) coconut oil, melted

Spicy barbecue sauce

40 g butter or ghee

600 ml tomato passata

200 g tomato paste

125 ml (½ cup) apple cider vinegar

80 ml (⅓ cup) maple syrup

80 ml (⅓ cup) coconut aminos (see Tip)

1 tablespoon garlic powder

1 tablespoon onion powder

1 tablespoon hot chilli powder

2 teaspoons freshly ground black pepper

1 teaspoon sea salt

Preheat the oven to 130°C and line a baking tray or roasting tin with baking paper.

Arrange the ribs on the prepared baking tray. In a bowl, combine all the spices with the salt and coconut oil to create a delicious basting paste. Rub this generously all over the ribs and bake for 3 hours, turning every 15 minutes, until the ribs are lightly golden and the meat is juicy and tender. Set the oven to grill at medium heat for the final 10 minutes of cooking to get the top of the ribs nice and crispy.

While the ribs are cooking, make the barbecue sauce. Melt the butter or ghee in a large saucepan, add the rest of the ingredients and whisk together until well combined. Bring to a gentle simmer and cook over low heat for 5 minutes, stirring occasionally, until the sauce has thickened and reduced slightly. Remove from the heat and transfer to a bowl or airtight container (the sauce will keep in the fridge for up to 5 days).

Remove the ribs from the oven, cover with foil and leave to rest for 5–10 minutes. To serve, transfer the ribs to a large serving platter and devour with the barbecue sauce. These ribs are great with Cauliflower Rice (see page 167), Mexican Red Cabbage Slaw (see page 136) or a simple green salad.

SERVES 4

See a pic of me on page 142

Wondering what I mean when I refer to coconut aminos? Well, it's a delicious and healthy sauce made from coconut sap. Sort of salty and slightly sweet in flavour, it resembles a light soy sauce but it is soy and gluten free, making it the perfect replacement for those following a paleo or clean-living lifestyle. It is available at most good health-food stores.

OVEN-BAKED
RIBS with SPICY
BARBECUE SAUCE
PAGE 140

CRISPY SKINNED PORK BELLY with BRUSSELS SPROUTS and BACON

Pork belly is hands down the thing I order most often when dining out. I absolutely love the crispy crackling combined with the tender, succulent meat underneath. I wanted to put this recipe in here so you don't have to eat out to enjoy such incredible flavours.

Preheat the oven to 220°C. Lightly grease a roasting tin with coconut oil.

Crush the fennel, coriander and cumin seeds using a mortar and pestle, then add the onion powder, garlic and coconut oil and pound together to form a lovely paste.

Score the skin of the pork belly by making 1 cm deep incisions with a sharp knife. Make three slightly deeper incisions, cutting through the fat completely, where you envisage dividing the belly into portions (this will make it easier to serve later).

Use your hands to rub the spice paste into the scored fat and all over the meat. Place the pork in the prepared tin, fill the tin with the water (making sure it doesn't touch the crackling) and season really well with salt and pepper. Roast for 10 minutes, then reduce the oven temperature to 160°C and cook for 1½ hours, checking it occasionally to make sure that the skin doesn't burn, until the meat is tender and cooked through and the crackling is crispy and golden. If the crackling isn't crackling yet, simply place it under the grill for a few minutes and it will begin to pop.

While the pork belly is cooking, get onto the brussels sprouts. Heat the coconut oil in a large frying pan over medium heat and sauté the brussels with the bacon and garlic until golden brown, crispy and delicious. Season with the salt.

Allow the pork belly to rest for 5–10 minutes, then cut through the deeper incisions to divide the belly into four pieces. To serve, simply arrange the pork belly pieces on a large platter together with the brussels sprouts and crispy bacon. Dig in.

SERVES 4

1 tablespoon fennel seeds

1 tablespoon coriander seeds

1 tablespoon cumin seeds

1 teaspoon onion powder

4 garlic cloves, crushed

3 tablespoons coconut oil, melted

1 x 800 g–1 kg pork belly

250 ml (1 cup) filtered water

sea salt and freshly ground black pepper

Brussels sprouts

2 tablespoons coconut oil, melted

500 g brussels sprouts, trimmed and halved

2–4 bacon rashers, cut into small pieces

2 garlic cloves, finely chopped

1 teaspoon sea salt

The use of fresh seeds in the spice rub leaves a charred top with epic crunch.

SLOW-ROASTED LAMB SHOULDER with CREAMY PARSNIP PUREE

I think if I were told I only had one meal left on this earth to enjoy, it would have to be a slow-cooked lamb shoulder. I simply cannot get enough. This is such an easy meal to prepare and is sure to wow anyone you serve it up for. Get planning and be sure to make it this Sunday!

1 x 2 kg lamb shoulder, bone in

2 teaspoons ground cumin

2 teaspoons ground coriander

2 teaspoons sweet paprika

sea salt and freshly ground
black pepper

2 tablespoons coconut oil

2 onions, roughly chopped

2 garlic cloves, roughly chopped

1 celery stalk, roughly chopped

2 carrots, roughly chopped

500 ml (2 cups) tomato passata

500 ml (2 cups) beef stock

2 thyme sprigs

2 rosemary sprigs

Parsnip puree

6 large parsnips (800–900 g),
cut into 2 cm cubes

125 ml (½ cup) coconut cream

sea salt and freshly ground
black pepper

Preheat the oven to 120°C.

Score the fat on the lamb shoulder all over with a sharp knife. Combine the cumin, coriander, paprika and plenty of salt and pepper and rub it into the lamb shoulder. Set aside.

Melt the coconut oil in a large, heavy-based saucepan over medium heat, chuck in the onion, garlic and celery and cook for 4–5 minutes, or until softened and caramelised. Add the carrot and cook for a further 5 minutes until slightly softened, then stir in the tomato passata, beef stock and fresh herbs. Season with a little salt and pepper and bring to the boil, then lower the heat to a simmer and cook for 10 minutes, or until thickened and reduced.

Lower the lamb, fat-side up, into a large casserole dish and pour over the sauce. Cover the dish with a lid, transfer to the oven and cook for 8–10 hours, or until the meat is meltingly tender. You'll know when it's ready because the meat will pull away from the bone really easily – if there's any resistance it may need a little longer.

When the lamb is almost ready, prepare the parsnip puree. Add the parsnip pieces to a saucepan of boiling salted water and cook for 15–20 minutes, or until soft and tender. Drain and leave to cool slightly, then tip into a bowl, add the coconut cream, season with salt and pepper and mash together until nice and smooth.

To serve, pull the lamb meat from the bone and divide among four plates. Spoon over some of the cooking juices and serve with the creamy parsnip puree.

SERVES 4

THINK and FEEL

How we think and feel can have a dramatic effect on how our lives play out, which makes it a major contributing factor to our health and happiness, not just on a daily basis but long term, too. If we can set our minds on the right positive path when we decide to change our lifestyle, then we put ourselves in good stead to be healthy both inside and out. I always say we must be healthy on the inside first to be truly healthy on the outside. You see, the power of the mind is an incredible thing, because the energy we put out into the universe is what we get back, so we can set our life path on a really positive direction just by utilising some simple happiness techniques, so that we think and feel the right stuff.

First up, how we think about ourselves is vitally important to our overall health and wellbeing. The more positive reinforcement that we can give ourselves – that we are good enough and that we are exactly where and who we are supposed to be – the more we alleviate a certain level of personal stress and self doubt and give ourselves the opportunity to thrive.

How we think about others is equally important, as this has a direct impact on all the relationships we have around us. The more we can interact with people coming from a place of love, support and humility, the more we can take down any barriers or blockages to happiness there may be in our world. When you offer others generosity, you will see it returned tenfold.

Feeling good starts with having the right mindset, so my advice is to start each day with a simple mantra that will remind you to live with love, intention and openness. It could be as simple as 'I will not judge myself or others. I will think, feel and act with love and be open to what this day brings.' True health starts from within, so look after your mind, and make it a happy one.

PERFECT STEAK with SWEET POTATO SHOESTRING FRIES

Some nights when I get home from a massive day or a big workout, my body just tells me it needs a steak to recover from the day. There's something sensational about a perfectly cooked steak with a simple side – take this standard pub fare to new places with this quick and easy recipe.

2 x 180 g beef fillet steaks

3 tablespoons coconut oil, melted

2 (about 300 g) sweet potato, cut into 3 mm matchsticks

To serve
bitter greens (I like rocket or baby kale)

Lime Aioli (see page 121)

Preheat the oven to 220°C and place the steaks on the bench so they have time to come to room temperature (never cook a steak straight out of the fridge – it's way too cold to hit the pan).

Heat 2 tablespoons of the coconut oil in a roasting tin over low heat, add the sweet potato pieces and mix together well, then transfer to the oven and cook for 20 minutes, or until nicely golden and crispy. Being so thin, the sweet potato fries will roast quickly, so keep an eye on them and give them a toss halfway through cooking.

While the fries are cooking, get started on the steaks. Heat the remaining 1 tablespoon of coconut oil in a frying pan over high heat until the oil is almost smoking (steaks should always be cooked over high heat, otherwise the meat will stew and go grey rather than caramelise to a lovely brown). Add the steaks to the pan and fry to your liking – 2 minutes on each side for rare, 2½ minutes for medium and (if you must) 3 minutes on each side for well done – only flipping them once during cooking. Remove the steaks from the pan, wrap them in foil and leave to rest for 2–4 minutes. Serve with the sweet potato fries, a handful of green leaves and a dollop of lime aioli

SERVES 2

SLOW-BRAISED BEEF CHEEKS
with CAULIFLOWER and GARLIC PUREE

My mum isn't a massive meat eater, but for some reason whenever she visits she requests my famous slow-cooked beef cheeks. I am touched that when she chooses to eat meat she chooses this, especially as I always make it with love to try and impress her.

Melt the coconut oil in a large, heavy-based saucepan or flameproof casserole dish over high heat. Season the beef cheeks generously with salt, add them to the pan and sauté for 3–4 minutes, or until sealed and browned on all sides. Remove the browned beef from the pan with a slotted spoon and set aside.

Utilising all the incredible juices that are now in your pan, add the onion, garlic and chilli and sauté for 3 minutes, or until soft and caramelised. Add the carrot and sweet potato and cook for a further 2 minutes, then pour over the tomato passata, tomato paste and beef stock. Stir through the bay leaf, thyme and rosemary and season to taste. Bring to the boil, then reduce the heat to very low, cover with a lid and simmer very gently for 5–6 hours, or until the meat falls apart when pressed with a fork.

For the cauliflower puree, steam or boil the cauliflower florets until soft, then transfer to a food processor with the butter or ghee, garlic and salt. Pulse until well combined and smooth.

Carefully remove the beef cheeks from the stew and set them aside, then crank the heat up to high. Bring the sauce to a simmer and cook until thickened and reduced to your liking, then return the beef cheeks to the sauce to warm through.

To serve, divide the cauliflower puree among four plates and garnish with a little chopped parsley. Spoon over the braised beef cheeks and sauce and serve.

SERVES 4

2 tablespoons coconut oil
4 x 220 g beef cheeks, trimmed
sea salt
1 onion, roughly chopped
4 garlic cloves, roughly chopped
1 long red chilli, deseeded and roughly chopped
2 carrots, roughly chopped
1 large sweet potato, roughly chopped
500 ml (2 cups) tomato passata
2 tablespoons tomato paste
750 ml (3 cups) beef stock
1 fresh or dried bay leaf
4 thyme sprigs
4 rosemary sprigs
freshly ground black pepper
chopped flat-leaf parsley leaves, to serve

Cauliflower and garlic puree

1 head of cauliflower, florets chopped and stalk removed
80 g butter or ghee
3 garlic cloves, grated
pinch of sea salt

Beef cheeks are a really tough piece of meat due to how much the animal uses these muscles. That's why slow cooking is the absolute best way to enjoy them. Slow cooking tougher cuts of meat such as veal shank and lamb shoulders can save you lots of money, as they are often much cheaper than the more expensive prime cuts.

GREEN CHICKEN CURRY with CAULIFLOWER RICE
PAGE 167

It's a tough call, but I think this dish could be my fave!

BAJA FISH TACOS with GUACAMOLE
PAGE 156

TAKEAWAY

Clean-eating twists on all your guilty pleasures

PALEO PIZZA with POACHED SALMON, ZUCCHINI and CAPERS
PAGE 161

BAJA FISH TACOS with GUACAMOLE

Last year I had the incredible opportunity of being the ambassador for Santa Monica. Part of what I learnt was that, being so close to the Mexican border, California has a sensational Mexican food culture, especially when it comes to street food. Every Friday night, food trucks would park along Marine Parade and serve real-deal stuff that had me smiling from ear to ear. One of those delights were real Baja fish tacos – here's my clean-living take on them.

130 g (1 cup) arrowroot flour

4 eggs, lightly beaten together with 3 tablespoons water

200 g (2 cups) almond meal

90 g (1 cup) desiccated coconut

600 g whiting, flathead or snapper fillets, skinned, pin-boned and cut into 8 pieces in total

sea salt

coconut oil, for deep frying

coriander leaves, to serve

lime cheeks, to serve

Guacamole

2 ripe avocados, mashed

1 garlic clove, grated

1 teaspoon ground cumin

1 teaspoon sweet paprika

finely grated zest and juice of 1 lime

1 small red chilli, deseeded and finely chopped

1 tablespoon extra-virgin olive oil

Soft tacos

3 tablespoons coconut oil, melted

3 tablespoons coconut flour

4 eggs, whisked

2 tablespoons extra-virgin olive oil

1 teaspoon baking powder

juice of ½ lime

1 teaspoon sea salt

Preheat the oven to 100°C.

To make the the guacamole, simply combine all the ingredients in a bowl and set aside.

For the tacos, whisk 1 tablespoon of the coconut oil with the flour, eggs, oil, baking powder, lime juice, salt and 170 ml (⅔ cup) of water in a large bowl. Leave to stand for 5 minutes to allow the batter to thicken.

Heat 2 teaspoons of coconut oil in a non-stick frying pan over medium–high heat. Pour 80 ml (⅓ cup) of the batter into the middle of the pan and, using the back of a spoon, spread out the mixture so it's nice and flat. Cook for 1 minute or so until firm enough to flip, then cook for 20 seconds on the other side. Repeat this process, adding a little more oil each time, to make eight soft tacos. Keep the tacos warm in the oven while you prepare the other ingredients.

Place the arrowroot flour in one bowl, the beaten egg mixture in another, and the almond meal and coconut in a third bowl. Season the fish pieces well with salt and dust lightly with the arrowroot flour, then dip them first into the egg mixture and then into the almond and coconut mixture to coat well.

Half-fill a large, heavy-based saucepan with coconut oil and set over medium heat. Heat the oil to 180°C. To test if it is hot enough, simply drop a small piece of bread into the oil – if it sizzles and bubbles you're good to go. Working in manageable batches, fry the fish for 90 seconds, or until golden and cooked through. Drain off any excess oil on paper towel and season with salt.

To assemble, simply load the warm tacos first with the guacamole, then top with the fish, a sprinkling of coriander leaves and a squeeze of lime juice.

SERVES 4

CRISPY FISH FINGERS and CHIPS with LIME AIOLI

When I was growing up, every Friday night was fish and chip night in my house. I remember heading down to the end of the street to pick them up, feeling the warmth of them through the bag and rushing home to get stuck in while sitting in front of *Burke's Backyard*. I want to share this version with you – which replaces the regular batter with a crispy quinoa and chia seed crumb – to replicate that same great taste without any of the naughty ingredients.

coconut oil, for deep frying

500 g (about 2) parsnips, peeled and cut lengthways into 1 cm thick chips

500 g (about 2) sweet potatoes, unpeeled and cut lengthways into 1 cm thick chips

sea salt and freshly ground black pepper

2 garlic cloves, grated

2 eggs

1 tablespoon finely grated lemon zest

½ teaspoon sea salt

1 teaspoon sweet paprika

300 g (2 cups) quinoa flakes

2 tablespoons white chia seeds

4 x 200 g whiting or snapper fillets, halved

lemon wedges, to serve

Lime Aioli (see page 121), to serve

Preheat the oven to 100°C.

Half-fill a large, heavy-based saucepan with coconut oil and set over medium heat. Heat the oil to 180°C. To test if it is hot enough, simply drop a small piece of bread into the oil – if it sizzles and bubbles you're good to go. Add the parsnip and sweet potato chips to the hot oil and fry for 4–5 minutes, or until cooked through and nice and golden (you may want to do this in batches depending on how big the pan is). Once cooked, transfer the chips to a paper towel to drain off any excess oil, then season and pop in the oven to keep warm.

Place the garlic, eggs, lemon zest, ½ teaspoon of the salt and the paprika in a bowl and mix together well. In a separate bowl combine the quinoa flakes and chia seeds. Dip the fish pieces first into the egg mixture and then into the flakes and seeds to coat.

Carefully lower the coated fish pieces into the hot oil and fry for 4–5 minutes, turning halfway through cooking, until golden brown and cooked through. Transfer to paper towel to drain off any excess oil. Serve with the chips, lemon wedges and lime aioli.

SERVES 4

What I love ...

Whiting provides about half of your recommended daily intake of vitamin B12, which supports healthy adrenal function, helps maintain a healthy nervous system, and is necessary for a number of key metabolic processes.

Wrap this meal up in paper and take it to the beach.

PALEO PIZZA with POACHED SALMON, ZUCCHINI and CAPERS

Who says you can't indulge in pizza when clean living? Certainly not me! Getting inventive with paleo staples such as cauliflower and almond meal gives us the opportunity to enjoy all the same great flavours of a home-delivered pizza, but with added health benefits in every bite.

Preheat the oven to 220°C and line a baking tray or pizza tray with baking paper.

Place the cauliflower, garlic, onion and salt in a food processor and whiz down to fine, rice-sized pieces. Tip the cauliflower mixture into a bowl with the eggs and almond meal, and stir well to combine. The mixture should be dough-like in consistency – if it's looking a little crumbly, simply add some more almond meal until it holds together well.

To make the pizza base, spread out the cauliflower 'dough' to a thickness of 15–20 mm across the baking tray in whatever shape you like, then bake for 15 minutes, or until it is lightly golden. Remove from the oven and reduce the temperature to 180°C.

Cover the pizza base with the sliced tomato and poached salmon chunks and dot with the cashew feta. Bake for a further 10 minutes, or until the edges of the base are golden brown and the toppings are cooked through. Remove from the oven and top with the zucchini strips, basil leaves, capers and dollops of the macadamia pesto. Drizzle over the olive oil and serve.

SERVES 4

1 head of cauliflower, florets and stalk roughly chopped

1 garlic clove, grated

½ onion, grated

pinch of sea salt

4 eggs

250 g (2½ cups) almond meal, plus extra if needed

4 roma tomatoes, sliced

400 g poached salmon fillets, skin removed and flesh flaked

2 tablespoons Cashew Feta (see page 79)

1 zucchini, cut lengthways into very thin strips

8 basil leaves, torn

1 tablespoon capers, rinsed

2 tablespoons Macadamia Pesto (see page 105)

1 tablespoon extra-virgin olive oil

SURF and TURF with ONION RINGS and HOMEMADE KETCHUP

For as long as I can remember I have been heavily involved with beach culture – from summer holidays as a kid to lifeguarding on Bondi Beach. Over the years, one thing I have seen in surf clubs across Australia is incredible surf and turfs! I couldn't share this book with you without putting this old favourite of mine in here.

2 garlic cloves, roughly chopped

½ teaspoon dried chilli flakes

1 teaspoon dried oregano

sea salt

2 tablespoons coconut oil, melted, plus extra for deep frying

4 x 220 g rib eye or fillet steaks

100 g (1 cup) almond meal

190 g (1½ cups) arrowroot or tapioca flour

2 teaspoons sweet paprika

250 ml (1 cup) canned coconut milk

4 egg whites

2 large onions, sliced into rings

8 large raw tiger prawns, peeled and deveined

Homemade ketchup (makes 250 ml/1 cup)

200 g tomato paste

1 tablespoon apple cider vinegar

1 teaspoon garlic powder

1 teaspoon onion powder

½ teaspoon sea salt

1 teaspoon honey

To serve

lemon wedges

garden salad

Lime Aioli (see page 121)

For the ketchup, put the tomato paste and 80 ml (⅓ cup) of water in a saucepan set over medium heat and stir together well. Add the remaining ingredients and stir to combine. Bring to the boil, then reduce to a simmer and cook for 15–20 minutes until thickened, adding a little more water if you want a runnier ketchup. Transfer to an airtight container and store in the fridge until needed (where it will keep for up to 2–3 weeks).

Using a mortar and pestle, pound the garlic, chilli flakes, oregano, 2 teaspoons of salt and 1 tablespoon of the coconut oil to make a delicious paste. Rub the paste over the steaks, making sure to coat all sides.

Heat the remaining 1 tablespoon of coconut oil in a large frying pan over high heat. Add the steaks and cook for about 3 minutes on each side for medium–rare. Transfer the steaks to a warm plate and leave to rest for 5 minutes.

While the steaks are resting, cook the onion rings and prawns. In a bowl, mix together the almond meal, arrowroot or tapioca flour, paprika and 1 teaspoon of salt, then add the coconut milk, egg whites and 125 ml (½ cup) of water and whisk together to form a batter. Dip the onion rings and prawns in the batter to coat.

Half-fill a large, heavy-based saucepan with coconut oil and set over medium heat. Heat the oil to 180°C. To test if it is hot enough, simply drop a small piece of bread into the oil – if it sizzles and bubbles you're good to go.

Using tongs, carefully lower the battered prawns and onion rings into the hot oil in batches. Cook for 1–2 minutes, or until golden brown, then remove from the oil and drain on paper towel.

Divide the steaks among four plates. Top each with two of the prawns and serve with the onion rings, ketchup, a few lemon wedges, a garden salad and some lime aioli.

SERVES 4

POPCORN CHICKEN with AVOCADO and MACADAMIA SALSA

Who doesn't love the crunch of crispy popcorn-style chicken? It was a bit of a staple of mine back in the days when I wasn't so clean living and before I understood what my poor food choices were doing to my wellbeing. That's why I've come up with this healthy popcorn chicken recipe, which contains all of the expected crunch and flavour without any of the unnecessary nasties.

60 g (½ cup) white chia seeds

45 g (½ cup) desiccated coconut

3 tablespoons almond meal

3 tablespoons arrowroot flour

3 teaspoons dried chilli flakes

3 teaspoons sweet paprika

3 teaspoons sea salt

2 teaspoons freshly ground black pepper

600 g chicken thigh fillets, roughly cut into thumb-sized pieces

2 egg whites, beaten

3 tablespoons coconut oil, melted

Avocado and macadamia salsa

3 avocados

240 g (1½ cups) toasted macadamia nuts

4 garlic cloves, grated

juice of 3 limes

2 bunches of basil, leaves picked

sea salt and freshly ground black pepper

Preheat the oven to 180°C and line a large baking tray with baking paper.

In a large bowl, mix together the chia seeds, desiccated coconut, almond meal, arrowroot flour, dried chilli flakes, paprika, salt and pepper until well combined.

Coat the chicken pieces in the beaten egg white and then toss them in the coating ingredients until really well covered. (It's best to do this in two or three batches to ensure you get an even coating.)

Arrange the coated chicken pieces on the prepared baking tray in a single layer and drizzle with the coconut oil. Bake for about 15–20 minutes, turning halfway through cooking, until crispy, golden brown and cooked through.

Meanwhile, prepare the avocado and macadamia salsa by pulsing all the ingredients in a food processor until well combined. Season to taste.

Pile the popcorn chicken into a serving bowl and serve with the salsa for dipping.

SERVES 4

This avocado and macadamia salsa also makes a great dip for sweet potato chips (see page 135) or finely chopped raw vegetables.

GREEN CHICKEN CURRY with CAULIFLOWER RICE

I am such a huge fan of spicy food, and what I love about Thai food is the way the different spices combine with the richness of coconut cream to create smooth, flavoursome curries. This one won't disappoint, so next time you are about to order from the local takeaway Thai joint, give it a go first.

Get started by making the green curry paste. Put all the ingredients in a food processor with 3 tablespoons of water and blitz to form a nice, smooth paste.

Heat the coconut oil in a saucepan over medium heat, add the curry paste and fry until nice and fragrant, stirring gently as it bubbles to prevent it from sticking to the pan.

Reduce the heat to low, add the coconut cream and the chicken stock or water and bring to a simmer. Add the chicken, kaffir lime leaves, capsicum, zucchini and bamboo shoots and simmer, stirring occasionally, for 15 minutes, or until the chicken is just cooked.

Meanwhile, make the cauliflower rice. Place the chopped cauliflower in a food processor and pulse briefly into tiny rice-like pieces. This usually takes about six to eight pulses. Melt the coconut oil in a large frying pan over medium heat, add the cauliflower rice and sauté for 4–6 minutes, or until softened. Season with salt to taste.

Remove the curry from the heat and stir through the water chestnuts, Thai basil and freshly chopped coriander. Serve with the cauliflower rice and lime cheeks (if using).

SERVES 4

Cauliflower is such a versatile vegetable and can be used in so many different ways to complement a clean-living lifestyle. This rice is great with curries and hearty braises – you can give it a flavour boost by adding fresh herbs, spices or even finely sliced vegetables. To turn the cauliflower rice into cauliflower couscous, simply pulse it in the blender for twice as long until very fine.

2 tablespoons coconut oil
400 ml coconut cream
125 ml (½ cup) chicken stock or filtered water
600 g chicken thigh fillets, roughly chopped
5 kaffir lime leaves
1 green capsicum, deseeded and cut into thin strips
2 zucchini, sliced into rounds
3 tablespoons canned bamboo shoots, drained
3 tablespoons canned water chestnuts, drained
1 large bunch of Thai basil, leaves picked
1 handful of coriander leaves, roughly chopped
lime cheeks, to serve (optional)

Green curry paste

5 spring onions, finely chopped
5 long green chillies, finely diced
5 garlic cloves, roughly diced
2 lemongrass stalks, white part only, chopped
5 cm piece of ginger, peeled and chopped
1 teaspoon ground coriander
1 teaspoon ground cumin
1 bunch of coriander, roots, stems and leaves chopped
1 tablespoon sugar-free fish sauce
juice of ½ lime
1 tablespoon honey
2 teaspoons sea salt

Cauliflower rice

1 head of cauliflower, florets and stalk roughly chopped
2 tablespoons coconut oil
pinch of sea salt

BEST CHICKEN PARMA with PARSNIP CHIPS and SALSA

I've always thought of an epic chicken parma as something to be enjoyed at a seaside pub overlooking the water, with a nice cool refreshment in hand. However, seeing as I am no longer a drinker, and don't normally eat the regular parma ingredients, I've had to create my own crowd-pleasing paleo version. Sparkling water on the side works a treat!

4 x 150 g chicken thigh fillets

sea salt and freshly ground black pepper

2 eggs, beaten

100 g (1 cup) almond meal

3 tablespoons arrowroot or tapioca flour

1 teaspoon dried oregano

1 teaspoon garlic powder

1 teaspoon sweet paprika

3 tablespoons coconut oil or duck fat

4 thick-cut slices of ham

200 g (1 cup) Tomato Salsa (see page 180)

80 g (½ cup) Cashew Feta (see page 79)

basil leaves, to serve (optional)

Parsnip chips

4 large parsnips, trimmed and cut into thick batons

2 tablespoons coconut oil, melted

1 teaspoon smoked paprika

½ teaspoon sea salt

Preheat the oven to 180°C. Line a baking tray with baking paper.

Place the chicken thigh fillets between two sheets of plastic wrap. Using a rolling pin or mallet, bash the thighs out into flat escalopes about 2–3 cm thick. Season with salt and pepper.

Place the beaten egg in a shallow bowl. In a second bowl, mix together the almond meal, arrowroot or tapioca flour, oregano, garlic powder, paprika and a pinch of salt. Dip each flattened chicken thigh first into the beaten egg and then into the almond meal mixture to coat evenly. Set aside.

To make the parsnip chips, mix the parsnip batons with the coconut oil, paprika and salt in a bowl. Spread the parsnip pieces out onto the prepared baking tray in a single layer and bake for 45 minutes, or until golden brown.

Now get started on the parmas. Melt the oil or fat in a large, deep frying pan over medium heat. Add the coated escalopes, in batches, and cook for 2 minutes on each side, or until brown and crispy, then remove from the pan and place on the prepared baking tray. Lay a slice of ham over each escalope and top with a generous dollop of the tomato salsa, then crumble over the cashew feta.

Bake the parmas for 5–10 minutes, or until the chicken is cooked through and the cashew feta is lightly golden. Divide the parmas among four plates, scatter over a few basil leaves (if using) and serve with the parsnip chips.

SERVES 4

CHICKEN SAAGWALA

I was first introduced to this when I found an incredible paleo Indian restaurant in Brisbane called It's Mirchi. I couldn't believe their whole menu was gluten, dairy and refined sugar free! This particular dish sparked my attention because of the spinach, which wilts down to create a rich, tasty curry. I believe one serving of this will give you more greens than most of us have in a whole day.

Melt the coconut oil in a large frying pan over medium heat. Add the cinnamon stick, cardamom pods, bay leaf and star anise and fry for 3–4 minutes, or until the whole spices begin to crack and release their incredible aromas.

Add the onion to the pan and cook for 5 minutes, or until soft and caramelised, then add the garlic and ginger and cook for another 5 minutes. Add the tomato passata, tomato paste and 3 tablespoons of water and stir in the chicken and ground spices. Bring to a simmer and cook for 15–20 minutes or until the chicken is cooked through. Remove from the heat.

For the spinach sauce, melt the coconut oil in a saucepan over medium heat. Add the spinach, cumin seeds and garlic and cook for 3–4 minutes, or until the spinach leaves have wilted.

Tip the spinach mixture into a food processor or blender and whiz until smooth.

Stir the spinach and the coconut cream into the curry and return the pan to the heat for a few minutes to warm through if needed. Serve with cauliflower rice.

SERVES 4

See a pic of me on page 173

2 tablespoons coconut oil

1 cinnamon stick

6 cardamom pods

1 bay leaf

2 star anise

4 onions, finely chopped

1 teaspoon finely chopped garlic

1 teaspoon finely chopped ginger

500 ml (2 cups) tomato passata

50 g tomato paste

1 kg boneless chicken thigh fillets, cut into large chunks

1 teaspoon garam masala

2 teaspoons ground coriander

2 teaspoons ground cumin

1 teaspoon chilli powder

1 teaspoon sweet paprika

3 tablespoons coconut cream

Cauliflower Rice (see page 167), to serve

Spinach sauce

2 tablespoons coconut oil

450 g baby spinach leaves

1 teaspoon cumin seeds

3 garlic cloves, chopped

TANDOORI
CHICKEN
DRUMSTICKS with
GREEN CHUTNEY
PAGE 175

SUPER-SPICY
BEEF VINDALOO
PAGE 174

CHICKEN
SAAGWALA
PAGE 171

SUPER-SPICY BEEF VINDALOO

Not for the faint hearted, this recipe is a real curry lover's paradise! I LOVE chilli, and I especially love them when they're hot. This clean-living beef vindaloo is everything a beautiful beef curry should be – I hope you enjoy it too.

800 g gravy beef or chuck steak, trimmed and cut into 4 cm cubes

juice of 1 lemon

2 cm piece of ginger, peeled and finely grated

1 tablespoon coconut oil

1 onion, chopped

3 garlic cloves, finely sliced

3 tomatoes, finely chopped

2 long green chillies, halved lengthways

125 ml (½ cup) apple cider vinegar

sea salt and freshly ground black pepper

1 handful of coriander leaves

Cauliflower Rice (see page 167), to serve

Spice mix

2 teaspoons hot chilli powder

1 teaspoon ground cumin

1 teaspoon ground coriander

1 teaspoon garam masala

1 teaspoon freshly ground black pepper

1 teaspoon ground cinnamon

1 teaspoon ground turmeric

For the spice mix, combine all the ingredients in a small bowl.

Place the beef, lemon juice and fresh ginger in a large bowl, tip over the spice mix and combine everything really well. Cover with plastic wrap, transfer to the fridge and leave to marinate for 1 hour.

When ready to cook, melt the coconut oil in a heavy-based flameproof casserole dish or a deep frying pan over medium heat. Add the onion and cook for 4–5 minutes, or until soft and caramelised, then add the garlic and cook for 2–3 minutes until fragrant.

Remove the beef pieces from the marinade and chuck them into the pan. Cook, stirring, for 8–10 minutes or until browned all over. Add the tomato, chilli, apple cider vinegar and 250 ml (1 cup) of cold water, increase the heat to high and bring almost to the boil. Lower to a simmer, cover and cook for 1½ hours, or until the sauce has thickened and the flavours have really developed. Season with salt and pepper to taste.

Divide the vindaloo among four plates, scatter over the coriander and serve with cauliflower rice.

SERVES 4

See a pic of me on page 172

Gravy beef is perfect for this type of dish. A very tough cut of meat, it really tenderises – becoming soft and gelatinous – when cooked over a long period of time.

TANDOORI CHICKEN DRUMSTICKS with GREEN CHUTNEY

A selection of clean-eating takes on Indian food would not be complete without some tandoori chicken! A staple at all Indian restaurants, my version takes out the yoghurt and utilises the goodness of coconut cream. Served alongside the green chutney, it's a flavour match made in heaven.

To make the spice paste, mix all the ingredients together in a bowl.

For the tandoori marinade, place all the ingredients in a food processor and blitz together until nice and smooth.

Using a super sharp knife, make two deep incisions in each drumstick, then press the spice paste into these incisions. Place the drumsticks in a bowl, pour over the marinade and mix together with your hands until all the drumsticks are evenly coated. Cover with plastic wrap, transfer to the fridge and leave to marinate for about 30 minutes, bringing the drumsticks back to room temperature before cooking.

Preheat the oven to 200°C. Line a large baking tray with baking paper.

When ready to cook, arrange the drumsticks on the prepared baking tray and roast for 20 minutes, turning slightly every 5 minutes until charred on the outside and tender and cooked through.

Meanwhile, make the green chutney. Place all the ingredients in a food processor or blender and whiz for 15–30 seconds to form a chunky paste.

Pile the delicious chicken drumsticks onto a large serving platter and serve with the green chutney.

SERVES 4

See a pic of me on page 172

1.5 kg chicken drumsticks, skin removed

Spice paste

1 teaspoon sea salt

1 teaspoon sweet paprika

1 teaspoon dried chilli flakes

finely grated zest and juice of 1 lime

Tandoori marinade

5 cm piece of ginger, peeled and roughly chopped

6 garlic cloves, grated

finely grated zest and juice of 1 lime

125 ml (½ cup) coconut cream

1 tablespoon ground coriander

1 tablespoon ground cumin

1 teaspoon ground fennel

1 teaspoon ground cardamom

1 teaspoon ground cloves

1 teaspoon sweet paprika

1 teaspoon cayenne pepper

1 teaspoon sea salt

2 tablespoons coconut oil, melted

Green chutney

1 salad onion bulb, roughly diced

1 bunch of mint, leaves picked

1 bunch of coriander, leaves picked

1 small hot green chilli

finely grated zest and juice of 1 lemon

½ teaspoon sea salt

1 teaspoon coconut nectar or maple syrup

SPICY PALEO PORK BURRITOS with RED CABBAGE SALAD

I think you're starting to see how much I love Mexican food! It's so fresh, zesty and packed full of flavour but is also really quick and easy food to prepare for the whole family. That's a win-win in my book.

3 tablespoons coconut oil

1 tablespoon ground paprika

1 tablespoon ground cumin

1 tablespoon chilli powder

1 x 400 g pork tenderloin fillet

100 g cherry tomatoes, quartered

1 red onion, finely diced

1 garlic clove, finely diced

1 avocado, mashed

½ bunch of coriander, leaves picked and roughly chopped

juice of 1 lime

Red cabbage salad

¼ red cabbage, outer leaves removed, finely shredded

juice of 1 lime

2 tablespoons apple cider vinegar

Tortillas

8 eggs

130 g (1 cup) tapioca or arrowroot flour

3 tablespoons coconut flour

pinch of sea salt

Preheat the oven to 100°C.

For the red cabbage salad, put the shredded cabbage in a bowl, pour over the lime juice and apple cider vinegar and mix together well. Cover with plastic wrap and place in the fridge for 30 minutes for the cabbage to soften.

For the tortillas, put all the ingredients in a food processor with 250 ml (1 cup) of water and whiz together to form a smooth batter.

Melt 1 teaspoon of the coconut oil in a frying pan over medium heat. Ladle 125 ml (½ cup) of the batter into the pan and spread it out into a circle about 20 cm in diameter with the back of a spoon. Cook for 2–3 minutes on each side until lightly golden, then transfer to the oven to keep warm. Repeat the process with the remaining batter, adding another 1 teaspoon of coconut oil each time, to make eight tortillas in total.

Mix together the paprika, cumin and chilli powder in a bowl, add the pork fillet and rub all over in the spice mixture to coat well. Melt the remaining 1 tablespoon of coconut oil in a large frying pan over medium heat, add the pork fillet and cook, turning regularly, for 8–10 minutes, or until the pork is golden and caramelised on the outside and juicy, tender and just cooked through on the inside. Remove the pork from the pan and leave to rest for 5 minutes before slicing it into thin rounds.

While the pork is resting, add the tomato, onion and garlic to the same pan and cook in the pork juices for 5 minutes, or until the onion has softened. Tip the mixture into a bowl and set aside.

To serve, divide the tortillas among four plates. Top each wrap with red cabbage salad, pork fillet slices, mashed avocado and the tomato and onion mixture, then scatter over the chopped coriander leaves and squeeze over the lime juice. Wrap everything up and you're good to go!

SERVES 4

See a pic of me on page 179

Good health starts
in the kitchen, with
real food.

SPICY PALEO
PORK BURRITOS
with RED CABBAGE
SALAD
PAGE 176

SWEET POTATO and CELERIAC NACHOS with THE LOT

I've said it before and I will say it again, I cannot get enough of Mexican food – it's full of incredible flavours that enliven the palate. These nachos are perfect for enjoying all year round.

2 sweet potatoes (about 300 g), peeled and sliced into very thin discs

2 celeriac (about 450 g), peeled and sliced into very thin discs

80 ml (⅓ cup) coconut oil, melted

1 teaspoon sweet paprika

sea salt

Guacamole (see page 156), to serve

Cashew Feta (see page 79), to serve

coriander leaves, to serve

Mexican beef chilli

2 tablespoons coconut oil

1 onion, finely chopped

3 garlic cloves, finely chopped

1 long red chilli, chopped

600 g beef mince

1 teaspoon ground cumin

1 teaspoon ground coriander

1 tablespoon tomato paste

1 x 400 g can diced tomatoes

Tomato salsa

4 roma tomatoes, deseeded and diced

½ red onion, finely diced

1 teaspoon sweet paprika

½ teaspoon dried chilli flakes

1 handful of coriander leaves, chopped

finely grated zest and juice of 1 lime

2 tablespoons extra-virgin olive oil

sea salt and freshly ground black pepper

Preheat the oven to 200°C and line two baking trays with baking paper.

Place the sweet potato and celeriac slices in a bowl with the coconut oil, paprika and salt and mix together well. Arrange the coated vegetable slices on the prepared baking trays in a single layer and bake for 10–15 minutes until crispy and golden brown. Set the veggie slices aside on paper towel to cool.

For the Mexican beef chilli, melt the coconut oil in a large frying pan over medium–high heat and sauté the onion, garlic and chilli for 3–4 minutes, or until tender and caramelised. Add the beef mince, break it up with a wooden spoon and brown off evenly, then stir in the spices, tomato paste and canned tomatoes and simmer for 10 minutes, or until the sauce has thickened and the flavours are well combined. Set aside.

For the tomato salsa, place all the ingredients in a bowl and mix together well. Season with plenty of salt and pepper.

To serve, tip the cooked vegetable crisps onto a large sharing platter, spoon over the beef chilli, guacamole and salsa and top with the cashew feta. Finish with a sprinkling of coriander leaves. All hands in!

SERVES 4

ZAGHETTI and MEATBALLS

I couldn't help but sing *La La La La La La La Bamba, Spaghetti and Meatballs* the whole time I wrote this recipe for you guys. I recommend you do the same when whipping up this incredible dish that the whole family is going to love! Entertain with your food AND your singing.

600 g beef mince

1 onion, grated

1 teaspoon dried oregano

1 teaspoon dried basil

1 egg

2 tablespoons almond meal

4 garlic cloves, grated

1 long red chilli, finely chopped

2 tablespoons coconut oil

750 ml (3 cups) tomato passata

1 small handful of basil leaves

Zaghetti

4 large zucchini

2 tablespoons extra-virgin olive oil

finely grated zest and juice of
1 lemon

pinch of sea salt

In a large bowl, combine the beef mince, onion, oregano, basil, egg, almond meal and half the garlic and chilli. Mix everything together really well with your hands until it feels as though the meat is binding together with the other ingredients, then roll into balls a little larger than golf balls.

Melt the coconut oil in a large, deep frying pan over medium heat, add the meatballs and cook for about 4–5 minutes, or until browned on all sides. Remove from the pan and set aside.

Add the remaining garlic and chilli to the pan and cook for 2–3 minutes, or until the garlic is caramelised and soft. Pour over the tomato passata and bring to the boil, then lower the heat to a simmer. Add the meatballs to the sauce and cook over low heat for 5–8 minutes, or until the meatballs are cooked through.

Meanwhile, make the zaghetti. Using a mandoline or sharp knife, cut the zucchini into long, thin strips, then cut each strip lengthways into spaghetti-sized pieces. Bring a saucepan of water to the boil, add the zucchini pieces and cook for 30 seconds, or until tender. Drain and transfer to a bowl, then toss through the olive oil, lemon zest, lemon juice and salt.

Divide the zaghetti among four serving bowls. Spoon over the meatballs and rich tomato sauce and scatter over the basil leaves to finish.

SERVES 4

If you have a spiraliser you can use it to make the zucchini noodles for this recipe. Feeling like mixing things up? Why not try using different coloured zucchini for this dish. The market near my place sells the most amazing yellow zucchini and they look great on the plate!

BACON and CHORIZO MEATZZA

Do you want to know what takes pizza to that next, epic level? Taking the traditional bread base and turning it into meat, that's what. What does this give you? The Meatzza. It's perfect for all those carnivores out there who find they just can't get a big enough protein hit.

Get started by preheating the oven to 230°C and lining a baking tray – or a pizza tray if you've got one – with baking paper.

To make the meatzza base, place all the ingredients in a bowl. Using your hands, mix everything together until really well combined.

Tip the beef mixture onto the prepared tray and use your hands to spread it out evenly in the shape of a circle. Bake for 8–10 minutes, or until cooked through. Remove the tray from the oven and drain off any excess liquid.

Using the back of a spoon, spread the passata evenly over the meat base and top with the bacon, chorizo, cherry tomatoes, chilli and olives. Return to the oven and cook for another 10 minutes, or until the base is lightly brown and the toppings are cooked through.

To serve, scatter over the basil and rocket leaves, drizzle over a little olive oil and cut into rough wedges.

SERVES 4

You can play around with the toppings on this one and even do a 100 per cent veggie topping to balance out the meaty base. Any leftovers can be kept in an airtight container in the fridge for up to 2 days and enjoyed cold.

3 tablespoons tomato passata

2 bacon rashers, roughly chopped

60 g (¼ cup) finely diced chorizo

8 cherry tomatoes, halved

½ red chilli, finely chopped

8 kalamata olives, pitted

6 basil leaves, roughly chopped

1 handful of rocket leaves

extra-virgin olive oil, to serve

Meatzza base

500 g beef mince

2 egg yolks

¼ onion, finely diced

2 garlic cloves, crushed

1 tablespoon finely chopped flat-leaf parsley leaves

½ teaspoon dried oregano

2 tablespoons almond meal

pinch of sea salt

pinch of freshly ground black pepper

US-STYLE BEEF and BACON SLIDERS

I love travelling to the United States. In LA and New York especially, there is this incredible food culture, from fine dining to authentic street food, and if there is one thing the Americans do right, it's a beef burger! I wanted to put this recipe together for you, because to me it has all the trimmings, from a juicy, succulent burger patty to an addictive barbecue sauce with a bite.

1–2 tablespoons coconut oil

4 bacon rashers

2 onions, sliced into rings

4 eggs

Buns

150 g (1½ cups) almond meal

100 g unsalted butter, melted

1 tablespoon white chia seeds

1 teaspoon baking powder

6 eggs, whisked

Patties

500 g beef mince, extra fatty if possible

½ onion, finely diced

1 egg

2 tablespoons finely chopped flat-leaf parsley leaves

2 garlic cloves, crushed

½ teaspoon dried chilli flakes

1 teaspoon sea salt

1 teaspoon freshly ground black pepper

To serve

Spicy Barbecue Sauce (see page 140)

Lime Aioli (see page 121)

1 tomato, cut into 8 slices

4 gherkins, sliced

1 carrot, finely grated

8 butter lettuce leaves

8 thin slices of baby beetroot

Preheat the oven to 180°C. Grease a 12-hole muffin tin with a little coconut oil.

Get started on the buns by mixing the ingredients together in a bowl to form a smooth dough. Divide the dough into eight portions and divide among eight greased muffin holes. Bake for 15–20 minutes, or until cooked and golden.

For the patties, mix all the ingredients together in a bowl with your hands and shape into four even patties about the size of the burger buns.

Melt the coconut oil in a large frying pan or use it to brush a hot barbecue plate, add the patties and cook for 4 minutes, before flipping and cooking for a few more minutes until cooked through.

Meanwhile, fry the bacon and onion rings together in the same pan or on the barbecue plate until golden brown and caramelised. Once the patties are cooked, fry the eggs in the juice left in the pan or on the barbecue to your liking.

To serve, trim the buns slightly to form a flat surface. Add the patties to four of the buns, pile over the eggs, bacon and onion and top with the paleo barbecue sauce and all the other incredible fillings and condiments. Put the bun tops on and devour like a slider should be devoured.

MAKES 4 SLIDERS

See a pic of me on page 189

Baby beetroots can often be found in the fresh produce area of supermarkets, pre-peeled and stored in their natural juices – with no added sugar.

US-STYLE BEEF
and BACON SLIDERS
PAGE 186

COCONUT—
BERRY ROUGH
PAGE 196

BLACK
FOREST BIRTHDAY
CAKE with
COCONUT ICING
PAGE 214

CELEBRATE

Festive food that's
good for you

TIRAMISU
TO DIE FOR
PAGE 213

You won't believe
how quick and
simple these
recipes are.

SWEET and SPICY GINGERBREAD MEN

I'm not sure I've ever met someone who doesn't love the delicious combination of flavours you find in a gingerbread man. They look cute and taste amazing, so why not make this clean-living version this Christmas? Heck, why wait? Make a batch any time of year!

Preheat the oven to 160°C. Line two baking trays with baking paper.

In a bowl, mix together the almond meal, ginger, cinnamon, nutmeg and baking powder. Set aside.

Put the coconut oil, maple syrup, vanilla seeds, egg and salt in a food processor and whiz together until well combined.

Slowly add the combined dry ingredients to the food processor and pulse together to form a dough. Remove the dough from the food processor and shape into a ball, then roll it between two sheets of baking paper, using a rolling pin, to a thickness of 1 cm.

Transfer the dough to the refrigerator for 20 minutes to firm up, then cut into shapes using cookie cutters or a sharp knife.

Place the cut shapes on the prepared baking trays and bake for 20–25 minutes, or until nice and golden. Remove them from the oven and allow to cool slightly on a wire rack. You're good to go!

MAKES ABOUT 10

300 g (3 cups) almond meal
1 tablespoon ground ginger
2 teaspoons ground cinnamon
1 teaspoon ground nutmeg
½ teaspoon baking powder
3 tablespoons coconut oil, melted
2 tablespoons maple syrup
1 vanilla pod, split and scraped
1 egg
pinch of sea salt

Tips

These gingerbread men are even more phenomenal when covered with my raw chocolate (see page 96). Simply melt the chocolate ingredients, then dip the gingerbread men into the mixture (or spoon the mixture over) and refrigerate until set. Don't feel limited to just making gingerbread men here either, feel free to cut the dough into whatever shapes you like – I like to make gingerbread puppies.

SUPERFOOD
BIRTHDAY
CUPCAKES
PAGE 197

The healthiest kids'
party treats you can get.

COCONUT–
BERRY ROUGH
PAGE 196

COCONUT-BERRY ROUGH

All too often kids' party food is packaged, processed and highly refined sugary junk, but there's no reason why our little ones should have to consume foods that are not good for them when celebrating. This is a definite crowd pleaser that will have both kids and parents reaching for a second square!

Base

200 g (2 cups) almond meal

150 g unsalted butter

3 tablespoons coconut flour

1 egg

1 vanilla pod, split and scraped

1–2 tablespoons maple syrup
(optional)

Berry filling

150 g (1¼ cups) raspberries,
fresh or frozen and thawed

65 g (½ cup) blueberries, fresh
or frozen and thawed

1 tablespoon maple syrup

Coconut rough topping

180 g (2 cups) desiccated coconut

2 eggs

1 vanilla pod, split and scraped

Preheat the oven to 180°C and line a 20 cm square baking tin with baking paper.

For the base, mix together the almond meal, butter and coconut flour in a bowl. Stir in the egg, vanilla seeds and maple syrup, if using, and mix to form a wet dough. Press the dough onto the base of the prepared baking tray in an even layer and bake for 15 minutes, or until lightly golden brown. Set aside to cool.

While the base is cooling, crack on with the berry filling. In the food processor, pulse the raspberries, blueberries and maple syrup together until well combined. Set aside.

For the topping, mix together the coconut, eggs and vanilla seeds in a bowl until well combined.

To assemble, spread the berry filling evenly over the cooled biscuit base, then sprinkle the coconut rough mixture on top, compacting it slightly with your hands or the back of a spoon. Return to the oven and bake for 30 minutes, or until the coconut is golden and cooked through. Set aside to cool for 5–10 minutes, then cut into squares and serve.

MAKES 9

See a pic of me on page 195

SUPERFOOD BIRTHDAY CUPCAKES

You'd never imagine these little cupcakes are packed full of nutrient-rich vegetables, vitamins, minerals and superfoods! That's why I love them so much. A cupcake that looks like the most decadent and delicious treat you've ever tasted, with all the health benefits of ingredients like maca powder, carrot and zucchini. Plus, who would have thought you could make icing out of an avocado?

Start by preheating the oven to 180°C and lining a 12-hole muffin tin with paper cases.

Whisk the eggs in a bowl. Add the melted coconut oil and whisk together until well combined, then, while continuing to whisk, gradually add the coconut sugar, vanilla seeds, cacao, maca powder, purple carrot powder (if using), baking powder and salt. Stir in the almond meal, desiccated coconut and grated carrot and zucchini to form a batter.

Divide the batter among the paper cases and bake for 25 minutes, or until a skewer inserted into a muffin comes out clean. Set aside to cool for 20 minutes while you get on with the icing.

For the chocolate icing, place the avocado, cacao powder and maple syrup in a food processor and blend together, stopping to scrape down the sides once or twice, until smooth and creamy. Spread the icing over the cooled cupcakes (the icing will be very runny in warm temperatures, so chill it in the refrigerator or freezer to firm it up if needed). Transfer the iced cupcakes to the refrigerator until needed to keep everything firm and prevent the icing from melting.

MAKES 12

See a pic of me on page 194

4 eggs

170 ml (⅔ cup) coconut oil, melted

150 g (¾ cup) coconut sugar

2 vanilla pods, split and scraped

125 g (1 cup) cacao powder

1 teaspoon maca powder

2 tablespoons purple carrot powder (optional)

2 teaspoons baking powder

pinch of sea salt

100 g (1 cup) almond meal

3 tablespoons desiccated coconut

1 carrot, grated

1 zucchini, grated

Chocolate icing

1 ripe avocado

60 g (½ cup) cacao powder

125 ml (½ cup) maple syrup

Tip

Purple carrot powder (made – surprise, surprise – from purple carrots) can be found in most health-food stores. Purple carrots are known as the original carrot, with a high phytonutrient density that gives them their rich colour. They're a fantastic source of antioxidants and fibre.

SENSATIONAL SAUSAGE ROLLS

As a kid I had a favourite bakery that sold the most amazing sausage rolls. Still to this day, whenever I drive past, memories come flooding back of that incredible flavour. Even just the smell enlivens my senses. This recipe does all of those things to me too, but without the gluten!

400 g beef mince

½ onion, finely diced

1 garlic clove, grated

pinch of sea salt and freshly ground black pepper

1 teaspoon ground allspice

3 teaspoons dried dill

½ teaspoon finely chopped chives

1 carrot, grated

1 zucchini, grated

5 shiitake mushrooms

2 egg whites

Spicy Barbecue Sauce (see page 140), to serve

Pastry

200 g (2 cups) almond meal

2 eggs

3 tablespoons coconut oil, melted

¼ teaspoon baking powder

Preheat the oven to 170°C. Line a baking tray with baking paper.

For the pastry, combine the almond meal, eggs coconut oil and baking powder in a bowl and mix well to form a nice, wet dough. Refrigerate for 30 minutes and get started on the filling.

Combine the mince with the onion, garlic, salt, pepper, allspice, herbs and vegetables and mix really well. Add 1 egg white to bind the mixture and set aside.

Remove the pastry from the fridge and place it on some baking paper. Roll out using a rolling pin until 5 mm thick. Cut it lengthways into two rectangles. Divide the filling equally between the rectangles then roll them up, sealing the dough edges with the remaining egg white using a pastry brush. Slice each rectangle into six even pieces.

Place on the prepared tray, seam-side down, and bake for 35–40 minutes, or until the pastry is lovely and golden and the filling is cooked.

Serve with my spicy barbecue sauce.

MAKES 12

I didn't think it was possible, but I've done it: sausage rolls that taste better than the original!

CHOCOLATE NUT BUTTER-DIPPED BANANAS

Looking for a celebratory sweet treat that utilises the goodness of real fruit? Well, this recipe takes chocolate dipping to the next level. Move over strawberries, this recipe shows you how to pimp your bananas to make them fit for any party!

250 g (2 cups) Raw Chocolate (see page 96), melted

pinch of sea salt

3 large bananas, peeled and halved horizontally

120 g hazelnut or almond butter

1½ tablespoons cacao nibs

2 tablespoons toasted hazelnuts, crushed to a crumb

3 tablespoons shredded or desiccated coconut

Line a baking tray with baking paper.

Make the raw chocolate as per the instructions on page 96 until melted. Stir in the salt and set aside off the heat.

Insert a wooden icy pole stick into the cut end of each banana half. Cover the tip of each banana half in 1 tablespoon of the nut butter, then dip each of the banana halves into the melted chocolate until coated almost all the way to the handle. Place on the prepared baking tray.

Sprinkle the cacao nibs over two of the banana halves, the toasted hazelnuts over another two and the coconut over the final two halves. Place in the fridge or freezer until set and ready to eat.

MAKES 6

What I love ...

Bananas contain high levels of tryptophan, which is converted by the body into serotonin, the happy-mood neurotransmitter that can help to combat depression. They also make the perfect pre-workout snack, packing a powerful energy punch and helping sustain blood-sugar levels during exercise.

Tip

Feel free to cover these bananas in other favourite coating ingredients, such as crushed pistachio nuts, crumbled walnuts and freeze-dried raspberries.

REST and RECOVER

This is one of my absolute favourite clean-living pillars, and the one most often overlooked due to our often very busy, time-poor, switched-on lifestyles. In this day and age, adequate rest and recovery has never been more important. Everything from sleep and stretching to simply limiting screen time and looking out for ourselves is a huge priority if we are to live to our full potential and be the best versions of ourselves.

Resting can come in many forms. It can be as basic as getting enough sleep each and every night. I am an eight hours man and believe the hours before midnight are the best – I can certainly tell when I haven't had enough sleep as my emotions and judgement are affected. Resting can also mean taking time out from your training to give your body the chance recover and your muscles the opportunity to repair. Sometimes people overtrain and therefore overstrain their bodies in the pursuit of wellness, so make sure you listen to yours and understand how to nourish it in all ways. Importantly, resting can also mean taking some much needed time away from your tablet, smartphone or TV.

Resting allows our bodies and minds to return to normal working order, reduces fatigue and re-sets us, so to speak. So whether it be from exercise or life's busy stressors, I classify the act of resting as recovering from whatever life is throwing at you. One of the best things I have been taught is to eat, move and rest intuitively, to allow my body to tell me what I need and when I need it. That is true connection to who you really are.

Any leftover jam can be enjoyed with my breakfast loaves.

DARK CHOCOLATE LAMINGTONS with BLUEBERRY–CHIA JAM

You can't celebrate Australia Day without indulging in a lamington. Tart jam sandwiched between layers of sponge and all coated in mouth-watering chocolate – I can't see anything wrong with this picture. You'll notice I've recreated this Aussie classic with blueberry jam – thank me later. Aussie, Aussie, Aussie, Oi, Oi, Oi.

Preheat the oven to 160°C. Grease and line a 35 cm x 25 cm x 5 cm baking tray with baking paper.

In a bowl, mix together the coconut oil, maple syrup and vanilla seeds. In a separate bowl, beat the eggs with an electric hand-held whisk for 4 minutes, or until thick and airy. Continuing to whisk, slowly pour the coconut oil mixture into the eggs until incorporated, then gently fold in the baking powder, arrowroot or tapioca flour and almond meal with a spoon, being careful to keep as much air in the batter as possible.

Pour the cake batter into the prepared baking tray and bake for 25 minutes, or until a skewer inserted in the centre comes out clean. Turn the sponge cake out onto a wire rack and set aside to cool completely.

While the sponge is cooling, get on with the jam and icing. For the blueberry–chia jam, put all the ingredients in a small saucepan over medium heat and stir together with a spoon. Bring to the boil, then lower the heat to a simmer and cook for about 20 minutes, or until nice and thick. Set aside. (For a really smooth consistency you can pass the jam through a fine sieve, but I personally like mine a bit rustic, so I keep it as is.)

To make the dark chocolate and coconut icing, combine all the ingredients in a bowl. Whisk everything together for a minute or so until thick and creamy, then set aside until needed.

Now get onto assembling these delicious lamingtons. Neatly trim the edges and top of the cooled sponge cake to form an even rectangle, then cut the rectangle in half horizontally. Spread a thin layer of jam over one of the sponges then sandwich the two sponge layers together. Cut the sandwiched sponge into 15 squares.

To finish, submerge the sponge squares in the chocolate icing, then scatter over the coconut to coat evenly. Set aside on a wire rack for 1 hour for the chocolate icing to firm before serving, or store in the fridge until needed.

MAKES 15

250 ml (1 cup) coconut oil, melted

125 ml (½ cup) maple syrup

2 vanilla pods, split and scraped

8 eggs

2 teaspoons baking powder

130 g (1 cup) arrowroot or tapioca flour

200 g (2 cups) almond meal

120 g (2 cups) shredded or flaked coconut

Blueberry–chia jam

375 g (3 cups) blueberries, fresh or frozen and thawed

250 ml (1 cup) maple syrup

finely grated zest and juice of 1 lemon

40 g (¼ cup) chia seeds

Dark chocolate and coconut icing

200 ml coconut oil, melted

150 g (1¼ cups) cacao powder

2 vanilla pods, split and scraped

125 ml (½ cup) coconut cream

80 ml (⅓ cup) maple syrup

Tips

Have heaps of jam left over? Perfect! It's great to enjoy on all your other bakery items and sweet treats. Store in a sealed, sterilised jar and refrigerate until needed. It'll keep in the refrigerator for up to 3 months.

CHOCOLATE-CHIP HOT CROSS BUNS

Two of my favourite things at Easter time are chocolate and hot cross buns, so why not combine the two and give your tastebuds one hell of a party? These are incredible fresh out of the oven, ripped open and smeared with butter.

200 g (2 cups) almond meal

65 g (½ cup) coconut flour

125 ml (½ cup) maple syrup

6 eggs

1 tablespoon ground cinnamon

2 teaspoons ground nutmeg

250 ml (1 cup) coconut oil, melted

3 tablespoons cacao nibs

1 teaspoon ground allspice

finely grated zest of 1 orange

2 green apples, peeled and grated

2 tablespoons dried blueberries

Crosses

3 tablespoons coconut oil, melted

2 tablespoons maple syrup

2 tablespoons coconut flour

1 egg white

Preheat the oven to 180°C and line a 12-hole muffin tin with paper cases.

In a large bowl, combine the almond meal, coconut flour, maple syrup, eggs, cinnamon, nutmeg, coconut oil, cacao nibs, allspice and orange zest and mix everything together to form a wet dough. Gently stir in the grated apple and blueberries, then form the mixture into 12 balls. Place the balls in the prepared muffin cases and set aside.

For the crosses, combine all the ingredients in a bowl to form a smooth paste. Transfer the mixture to a piping bag, or a plastic sandwich bag with a corner cut off, and pipe the mixture over the surface of each dough ball in the shape of a cross.

Bake the buns for 25–30 minutes, or until nice and golden on top. Remove them from the oven and leave to cool on a wire rack. I store these in an airtight container in the fridge for up to 5 days, but good luck stopping at just one!

MAKES 12

See a pic of me on page 208

Not a fan of chocolate chips? Just leave the cacao nibs out of the batter. If you're looking to mix things up with your flavours, try adding different berries. Although not traditional, adding freeze-dried raspberries to this recipe in place of the blueberries works amazingly well.

CHOCOLATE-
CHIP HOT
CROSS BUNS
PAGE 206

NO-FUSS EASTER EGGS

No moulds or special equipment, no fuss and just a little bit of mess … these eggs are so easy and so delicious. Make them your perfect healthy go-to this Easter.

65 g (¾ cup) desiccated coconut

80 ml (⅓ cup) coconut oil, melted

3 tablespoons coconut cream

1 tablespoon maple syrup

1 vanilla pod, split and scraped

Chocolate coating

220 g cacao butter

120 g (1 cup) cacao powder

125 ml (½ cup) maple syrup or 175 g (½ cup) honey

1 vanilla pod, split and scraped

pinch of sea salt

Mix together the desiccated coconut, coconut oil, coconut cream, maple syrup and vanilla seeds in a bowl. Transfer to the freezer and leave to chill for 30 minutes, or until firm enough to shape.

Divide the mixture into 12 pieces. Using your hands, roll each piece into an egg shape. Arrange the eggs on a plate or tray and return to the freezer for 30 minutes to set completely.

While the eggs are chilling, make the chocolate coating. In a saucepan, melt the cacao butter over low heat, add the remaining ingredients and mix together to form a creamy, chocolatey sauce.

Dip the chilled coconut eggs into the chocolate coating to cover all over, then return to the fridge until set and ready to be devoured!

MAKES 12

TIRAMISU TO DIE FOR

I love coffee and I love dessert, so the classic tiramisu is a no-brainer for me. Bursting with flavour, this is the perfect after-dinner delight when entertaining. Make sure you prepare the components in advance to give yourself enough time for assembling and chilling.

Preheat the oven to 200°C. Line a large baking tray with baking paper.

For the ladyfinger biscuits, separate three of the eggs into two bowls. Using an electric hand-held whisk, whisk the egg whites on medium–low speed until frothy. Add the lemon juice and continue to whisk until stiff peaks form.

Add the remaining eggs to the egg yolk bowl, together with the maple syrup, vanilla seeds and salt, and whisk until pale and creamy. Add the coconut flour and baking powder and whisk together to form a batter. Carefully fold the beaten egg whites into the batter, then pour the mixture into a piping bag or a plastic sandwich bag with the corner cut off to create a nozzle. Pipe the batter onto the prepared baking tray in roughly 5 cm x 3 cm strips, being sure to leave 2 cm or so between each biscuit as they will spread while cooking. Bake for 10–12 minutes, or until almost golden, then remove from the oven and leave to cool completely.

To make the whipped coconut cream, scoop the solid set cream from the coconut cans into a bowl, being careful not to add any of the clear coconut liquid (keep this for smoothies!). Using a hand-blender on high speed, whisk the coconut cream until soft peaks form. Add the maple syrup and vanilla seeds and continue to whisk on high speed until firm peaks form.

To assemble the tiramisu, line a 22 cm loaf tin with plastic wrap. Arrange a third of the ladyfinger biscuits over the bottom of the tin and pour over a third of the espresso, then spoon over a third of the whipped cream to cover. Repeat this process twice more until you have three layers of each ingredient. Cover the tin in plastic wrap and refrigerate for at least 4 hours, ideally overnight, to firm up.

When ready to serve, uncover the tiramisu and lift it from the tin by pulling on the edges of the plastic wrap. Transfer to a serving plate, dust with the cacao powder and, if you like, scatter over some cacao nibs and roasted coffee beans.

SERVES 6

125 ml (½ cup) fresh espresso coffee, cold

2 tablespoons cacao powder

cacao nibs and roasted coffee beans, to serve (optional)

Ladyfinger biscuits

6 eggs, at room temperature

a squeeze of lemon juice

125 ml (½ cup) maple syrup

2 vanilla pods, split and scraped

pinch of sea salt

65 g (½ cup) coconut flour

½ teaspoon baking powder

Whipped coconut cream

2 x 400 ml cans coconut cream, chilled

2 tablespoons maple syrup

1 vanilla pod, split and scraped

For perfectly set coconut cream, simply place your cans upside down in the fridge the day before use. When you flip them over and open them, all the firm good stuff will be at the top, ready for you to scoop out and use.

BLACK FOREST BIRTHDAY CAKE with COCONUT ICING

When I was a kid I always wanted to have a black forest birthday cake, as I was such a fan of the original frozen version. Now here I am giving you a healthy version of my childhood dream – just don't forget to blow out the candles! Before you get started, be sure to have two 22 cm springform cake tins to hand – this beauty is double layered.

135 g (1 cup) coconut flour

90 g (¾ cup) cacao powder

½ teaspoon baking powder

½ teaspoon sea salt

10 eggs

185 ml (¾ cup) coconut oil, melted

185 ml (¾ cup) coconut water

2 vanilla pods, split and scraped

250 ml (1 cup) maple syrup

155 g (½ cup) blueberries, fresh or dried

250 g (2 cups) mixed berries, fresh or frozen and thawed (cherries and blackberries work best)

cacao nibs, to serve (optional)

Coconut icing (makes 600 g/3 cups)

300 ml coconut cream, chilled

300 g coconut yoghurt

75 g (⅓ cup) honey

1 vanilla pod, split and scraped

Get started by preheating the oven to 180°C and greasing and lining two 22 cm springform cake tins with baking paper.

Put the coconut flour, cacao powder, baking powder and salt into a stand mixer and mix together well. Turn the speed to low and add the eggs followed by the coconut oil in a long, slow drizzle until incorporated. Turning your mixer to high speed, add the coconut water, vanilla seeds and most of the maple syrup (reserve 2 tablespoons for the mixed berry topping). Reduce the speed again and add the blueberries until just combined, then finally return back to high speed until a smooth batter forms. (Note: this works best with a stand mixer but you could also use a hand-held electric mixer or work the batter thoroughly with a whisk by hand.)

Divide the cake batter evenly between the two prepared cake tins and smooth it out using the back of a spoon or a spatula. Bake for 25–30 minutes until a toothpick inserted in the centre of each sponge comes out clean. Leave to cool in the tins.

For the icing, put all the ingredients in your cleaned stand mixer and mix on medium speed for 5 minutes. Alternatively, you can use a hand-held electric mixer or a whisk and beat until smooth and creamy. Transfer the mixture to a bowl and refrigerate for 30 minutes.

Place the mixed berries in a bowl. Using a fork, gently mash them together with the remaining 2 tablespoons of maple syrup to break them up slightly and get some of the juices oozing.

Once the sponges are completely cool, use a knife to loosen the side of one of the tins and flip the sponge out onto a chopping board or cake plate. Spread a thick layer of coconut icing (about half of the mixture) over the sponge and spoon over half of the crushed berries. Remove the second sponge from its tin as before and place it on top of the first sponge, then spread over the remaining icing. Top with the remaining berries and scatter over the cacao nibs, if using.

SERVES 12

The cherries add such a beautiful texture to this cake.

BERRY RIPE FUDGE

Whether it's to share with friends at a dinner party or grab as you run out the door before training, this tart, gooey fudge is decadent, nutrient-dense and delicious. I just love simple, easy-to-prepare desserts, and this is one of the best.

100 g almond butter

100 ml coconut oil

60 g (½ cup) cacao powder

3 tablespoons maple syrup

1 vanilla pod, split and scraped

50 g blueberries, fresh or dried

Line a 35 cm x 25 cm baking tray with baking paper.

Put the almond butter, coconut oil, cacao powder, maple syrup and vanilla seeds in a food processor and blitz until really well combined. Spread the mixture evenly over the prepared baking tray and dot with the blueberries, fully submerging some and leaving others to sit nicely on the surface.

Transfer to the freezer for 30 minutes, or until set, then cut the fudge into chunky squares and you're good to go.

SERVES 6

PEANUT BUTTER CHEESECAKE BITES

Did someone say cheesecake and peanut butter? OK, you now have my full attention. This recipe combines two of my favourite things into easy-to-enjoy mouthfuls that look great and are perfect for entertaining. If you don't eat peanut butter, you can use any other type of nut butter instead.

Preheat the oven to 180°C and line a 20 cm square baking tin with baking paper.

For the base, mix together all the ingredients in a bowl to form a batter using an electric whisk. Spoon the batter into the prepared tray, being sure to cover the base evenly, and bake for 15 minutes, until golden brown. Remove from the oven and leave to cool for 15 minutes or so.

To make the filling, put all the ingredients in a food processor and pulse on high speed until smooth and creamy. Pour this mixture over the base, transfer the tray to the fridge and leave to chill and set for a minimum of 4 hours, or overnight for best results.

Once set, remove the cheesecake from the tray and cut it into 5 cm squares. Place the squares on a wire rack or a baking tray.

For the chocolate topping, melt the ingredients together in a saucepan over medium–low heat until nice and runny. Pour the melted topping over the cheesecake squares. Return to the fridge for 30 minutes for the topping to set before serving.

MAKES 16

Peanuts aren't actually nuts. They are legumes, which is why those following the paleo diet like to substitute them for other nut butters.

Base
100 g (1 cup) hazelnut meal

1 tablespoon coconut flour

½ teaspoon baking powder

pinch of sea salt

3 tablespoons coconut oil, melted

80 ml (⅓ cup) maple syrup

1 egg yolk

1 vanilla pod, split and scraped

Peanut butter cheesecake filling
100 g (1 cup) macadamia nuts, soaked for 2–4 hours or overnight, then drained and rinsed

125 ml (½ cup) Vanilla Almond Milk (see page 34) or Homemade Coconut Milk (see page 35)

125 ml (½ cup) maple syrup

125 ml (½ cup) coconut oil, melted

125 g peanut butter, or other nut butter

1 vanilla pod, split and scraped

pinch of sea salt

1 tablespoon gelatine powder, dissolved in 25 ml warm water

Chocolate topping
220 g cacao butter

120 g (1 cup) cacao powder

125 ml (½ cup) maple syrup or 175 g (½ cup) honey

1 vanilla pod, split and scraped

pinch of sea salt

CHRISTMAS FRUIT MINCE TARTS

Fruit mince tarts remind me of my amazing mum. Each and every Christmas when I walk through the door, I smell a fresh batch of locally made fruit mince tarts, which Mum always insists I sit down and enjoy with a warm cuppa and a long chat. For me, anything that reminds me of Mum and home is a good thing, so enjoy these beauties and share them with your own family and friends.

450 g (4½ cups) almond meal

100 g unsalted butter, chilled and cut into cubes

80 g (⅓ cup) coconut sugar

3 eggs

2 vanilla pods, split and scraped

125 ml (½ cup) Vanilla Almond Milk (see page 34)

1 egg white, beaten

coconut oil spray

Fruit mince

2 green apples, grated

finely grated zest and juice of 2 oranges

½ teaspoon ground allspice

½ teaspoon ground nutmeg

1 teaspoon ground cinnamon

85 g (⅔ cup) raisins

85 g (⅔ cup) sultanas

90 g (½ cup) dried apricots, finely chopped

50 g (1 cup) dried blueberries

For the fruit mince, mix all the ingredients together in a large bowl. Transfer to the fridge and leave to chill for 3 hours to allow the fruit to soak up all the delicious flavours.

While the fruit is soaking, get started on the pastry. Place the almond meal in a bowl, add the butter and rub it in with your fingertips until the mixture resembles fine breadcrumbs. Add the coconut sugar, eggs, vanilla seeds and almond milk, and mix everything together to form a soft dough. Cover in plastic wrap and leave to rest in the fridge for 1 hour.

Preheat the oven to 180°C and grease a 24-hole mini muffin tin with a little coconut oil.

Remove the pastry from the fridge and portion it into twenty-four 30 g balls, reserving any leftover dough. Flatten the balls into discs and gently press into the muffin holes. Press the pastry into the edges, making sure to cover the sides. Place the tray in the fridge for about 30 minutes. Remove and spray with some coconut oil and bake for 5–10 minutes, or until lightly golden.

Place a heaped tablespoon of the fruit mince mixture into each pastry case and either cover completely with more pastry or create a pattern. Brush the pastry with the beaten egg white and bake for 15–20 minutes or until beautiful and golden. Here, I have chosen to keep them as open tarts.

MAKES 24 TARTS

Leftover pastry? Use it to make shapes or patterns to top the tarts.

Love my morning coffee and treat chill time ...

APPLE
and RASPBERRY
NUTTY CRUMBLE
PAGE 228

NO-BAKE CACAO and RASPBERRY CAKE with CREAMY CHOCOLATE ICING
PAGE 239

SWEET

The tastiest treats you ever did eat

RAW CHOC-BERRY CHEESECAKE PAGE 242

PERFECT RASPBERRY and COCONUT MACAROONS

When I was a contestant on *My Kitchen Rules,* I fell in love with the combination of coconut and raspberries after scoring a 10 out of 10 with the first dessert I baked in the competition – a spelt raspberry macaroon tart. It was a hit with the judges and a hit with me. This is my quick and easy nod to that more elaborate dish.

300 g (4½ cups) shredded coconut

250 ml (1 cup) maple syrup

2 vanilla pods, split and scraped

pinch of sea salt

4 egg whites

125 g (1 cup) fresh or frozen raspberries

Preheat the oven to 160°C and line a large baking tray with baking paper.

In a food processor, briefly pulse 240 g (4 cups) of the shredded coconut together with the maple syrup, vanilla seeds, salt and egg whites to form a paste. Add the remaining shredded coconut and raspberries and pulse once or twice to combine, but not to break down the berries fully.

Spoon the mixture into macaroon-sized balls and arrange them on the prepared baking tray, leaving a gap of 2 cm between each ball. Bake for 25–30 minutes, or until the tops are nicely browned, then leave to cool on a wire rack before serving. The macaroons will keep stored in an airtight container in the fridge for up to 5 days.

MAKES ABOUT 24

See a pic of me on page 226

Tip

For an extra flavour hit, try dipping these in some melted raw chocolate (see page 96).

CHOC-ESPRESSO BITES

Chocolate and coffee! Possibly my two favourite flavours, though I actually think they are even better when they join forces. Stimulating, bitter and rich, these choc–espresso bites make the perfect treat or pre-workout energy hit.

70 g coconut butter
60 g (½ cup) cacao powder
1 tablespoon ground coffee
1 tablespoon shredded coconut
1 vanilla pod, split and scraped
3 tablespoons maple syrup
1 tablespoon coconut oil, melted
18 coffee beans

Line a 6-hole muffin tin with paper cases.

Gently soften the coconut butter in a saucepan over low heat (you want it to be just malleable when pressed with a fork), then add the cacao powder, ground coffee, shredded coconut, vanilla seeds, maple syrup and coconut oil. Stir together well until combined.

Pour the mixture evenly into the paper cases. Decorate each with 3 coffee beans, transfer to the freezer and leave for 1 hour to set. Enjoy straight from the freezer, or if you prefer a softer bite, leave them to sit at room temperature for 20 minutes before serving.

MAKES 6

See a pic of me on page 227

You can get really creative with this recipe – try adding a few finely chopped macadamia nuts or hazelnuts to the chocolate mixture for texture and crunch.

MATCHA GREEN-TEA BITES

Looking for a chocolatey energy hit that will have you both bouncing off the walls with energy *and* burning body fat? Well, look no further than these epic matcha green-tea bites. Cacao has been proven to give the body an antioxidant-rich stimulant kick, while matcha green tea is renowned for its fat burning properties. Eat chocolate, get lean. True story.

220 g cacao butter
125 ml (½ cup) maple syrup or 175 g (½ cup) honey
2 tablespoons matcha green tea powder
1 vanilla pod, split and scraped
pinch of sea salt
90 g (¾ cup) cacao powder

Melt the cacao butter together with the maple syrup or honey in a saucepan over very low heat. Stir in the matcha powder, vanilla seeds and salt, then remove the pan from the heat and whisk everything together until smooth and creamy.

Line a 12-hole muffin tin with eight paper cases. Pour half the melted mixture into the paper cases, being sure to fill each only halfway. Transfer to the freezer and leave for 15 minutes, or until firm.

Whisk the cacao powder into the remaining mixture over low heat until it is well combined and free of lumps. Remove the muffin tin from the freezer and spoon over the cacao mixture. Return to the freezer for 15 minutes to set and they'll be ready to go!

MAKES 8

See a pic of me on page 227

What I love ...

Matcha is known to contain powerful antioxidants, catechins and manganese, which help to counteract the effect of free radical damage to our cells. As well as boosting your energy, the natural caffeine matcha contains is thought to have thermogenic (fat burning) properties, which can help support weight management.

PERFECT RASPBERRY and COCONUT MACAROONS PAGE 224

Make a big batch to share with family and friends.

MATCHA
GREEN-TEA BITES
PAGE 225

CHOC-
ESPRESSO BITES
PAGE 225

APPLE and RASPBERRY NUTTY CRUMBLE

There's something sensational about the combination of toasted nuts with oven-baked fruit – you get that incredible soft texture from the fruit with the crunch when the spoon digs into the nut crumble. This recipe calls for apples and raspberries, but do try and experiment with it. Pears and strawberries also work well.

4 green apples, cored and cut into 4 cm cubes

1 vanilla pod, split and scraped

1 teaspoon ground cinnamon

½ teaspoon ground nutmeg

125 g (1 cup) raspberries, fresh or frozen and thawed

Whipped Coconut Cream, to serve (see page 213)

Nutty crumble

100 g (1 cup) almond meal

3 tablespoons coconut oil or 60 g unsalted butter, very cold

160 g (1 cup) macadamia nuts, roughly chopped

1 tablespoon shredded coconut

2 tablespoons pumpkin seeds

2 tablespoons maple syrup

Preheat the oven to 180°C.

Arrange the apple pieces in a medium–large pie dish and sprinkle over the vanilla seeds, cinnamon, nutmeg and 2 tablespoons of water. Cover with foil and bake for 20 minutes, or until the apple is soft, but still holding its shape. Remove from the oven, uncover and set aside.

For the crumble, mix together the almond meal and cold coconut oil or butter in a bowl with your fingertips until the mixture resembles fine breadcrumbs. Add the macadamia nuts, shredded coconut and pumpkin seeds and mix together well, then stir in the maple syrup.

Dot the raspberries evenly over the par-cooked apples then, using your hands, spread the crumble mixture over the top, making sure it covers everything evenly and there are no gaps.

Bake for another 10–15 minutes, or until the crumble topping is crunchy and golden. Serve warm with whipped coconut cream.

SERVES 4

EASY CHOCOLATE-CHIP ICE CREAM

Sometimes I have a craving for ice cream that won't go away! This indulgent treat is a no-fuss, low-mess option for all you clean eaters out there, and it doesn't need any fancy equipment to make.

1 x 400 ml can coconut cream

80 g (⅔ cup) cacao powder

3 tablespoons maple syrup

1 vanilla pod, split and scraped

2 tablespoons cacao nibs, plus extra to serve (optional)

To make the ice cream, simply combine the coconut cream, cacao powder, maple syrup and vanilla seeds in a food processor or blender and blend until smooth and creamy. Pour the mixture into a suitable container, stir in the cacao nibs and freeze for 4–6 hours, stirring every 30 minutes to prevent ice crystals forming.

This recipe is best served and enjoyed on the day of making, as it can sometimes become very firm if left for too long in the freezer. Don't forget to keep stirring it while it sets! Serve with an extra sprinkling of cacao nibs, if you like.

SERVES 8

What I love ...

Cacao nibs – pieces of cacao bean that have been roasted and hulled – are basically raw chocolate before anything has been added. They are packed with high levels of antioxidants and magnesium and, on their own, taste a bit like roasted coffee beans.

Celebrate food and treat yourself the clean way.

PALEO BANOFFEE PIE

This classic English dessert is normally laden with dairy and processed sugars. I wanted to give you guys a recipe that contains the same incredible flavours, but with my clean-living take on the ingredients. Here it is.

Preheat the oven to 180°C and line a 22 cm fluted tart or pie tin with baking paper.

Place the almond meal, eggs, chia seeds, maple syrup, coconut oil and 60 g of the coconut flour in a food processor and pulse to a nice dough-like consistency, adding a little extra almond meal if the mixture is too wet or a drizzle more coconut oil if it's too dry. Press the mixture evenly into the tin and bake for 10–15 minutes, or until golden brown. Remove from the oven and allow to cool while you prepare the remaining elements.

Blitz the mashed bananas, coconut butter, vanilla seeds and remaining coconut flour in the food processor until smooth and creamy. Spoon the mixture evenly over the cooked base and place in the freezer for 20 minutes to firm up.

While the filling is firming, make the topping. Melt the coconut oil in a saucepan over low heat together with the cacao, honey and salt. Mix together well.

Remove the tin from the freezer and pour over the topping, then decorate with the banana slices or discs and shredded coconut. Return to the freezer for 30 minutes for the topping to harden.

When ready to serve, remove the banoffee pie from the freezer and leave it for 5 minutes to soften enough to cut easily with a warm knife. Sprinkle over the cacao nibs and enjoy. Yum!

SERVES 6

50 g (½ cup) almond meal, plus extra if needed

3 eggs

1 tablespoon chia seeds

3 tablespoons maple syrup

2 tablespoons coconut oil, melted, plus extra if needed

70 g (½ cup) coconut flour

4 bananas, 2 mashed and 2 sliced in half lengthways and then halved (or just slice them into discs)

2 tablespoons coconut butter

1 vanilla pod, split and scraped

3 tablespoons shredded coconut

2 tablespoons cacao nibs

Topping

125 ml (½ cup) coconut oil

60 g (½ cup) cacao powder

2 tablespoons honey

pinch of sea salt

MEXICAN CHOCOLATE MOUSSE

This dairy-free version of the classic dessert uses cinnamon and cayenne pepper to enliven the tastebuds. I personally enjoy mine with a nice cup of almond milk coffee and a good book. This is my mum's favourite dessert!

1 x 400 ml can coconut cream

125 ml (½ cup) maple syrup

1 vanilla pod, split and scraped

1 tablespoon gelatine powder

60 g (½ cup) cacao powder, plus extra to serve

2 teaspoons ground cinnamon

pinch of cayenne pepper

½ teaspoon ground nutmeg

pinch of sea salt

Combine the coconut cream, maple syrup and vanilla seeds in a saucepan over medium–low heat. When warm, tip 3–4 tablespoons of the mixture into a bowl with the gelatine and stir to dissolve, then return to the pan with the rest of the coconut cream mixture.

Add the coconut cream mixture to a food processor with all the remaining ingredients and blend together until light and fluffy.

Divide the mousse mixture between two small bowls or ramekins and leave to chill in the fridge for at least 20 minutes until set. Sprinkle with a little extra cacao powder before serving.

SERVES 2

BEST-EVER SALTED CARAMEL SLICE

The past few years have seen the combination of salt and caramel rocket off into the trendy stratosphere, partly thanks to the rise in food sharing on social media. So very hot right now, it's a must-have in your cooking repertoire.

Base

50 g (½ cup) pecans

50 g (½ cup) almond meal

4 medjool dates, pitted and soaked

3 tablespoons coconut oil, melted

1 tablespoon honey

Caramel filling

180 g medjool dates, pitted and soaked

65 g macadamia or cashew butter

125 ml (½ cup) Vanilla Almond Milk (see page 34)

125 ml (½ cup) coconut oil, melted

1 teaspoon ground cinnamon

pinch of sea salt

Topping

125 ml (½ cup) coconut oil, melted

60 g (½ cup) cacao powder

2 tablespoons honey

pinch of sea salt

Line a 30 cm x 20 cm high-edged baking tray with baking paper.

For the base, pulse all the ingredients in a food processor to a crumb-like consistency. Spread evenly over the prepared tray and transfer to the freezer to firm up.

For the caramel filling, put all the ingredients in the food processor and blitz everything together for 4 minutes, or until really smooth. Remove the tray from the freezer, pour over the date mixture and return to the freezer to firm up again.

For the topping, place all the ingredients in the food processor and blend for 1–2 minutes, or until smooth and chocolatey.

Remove the baking tray from the freezer again, pour over the chocolate mixture and spread evenly using the back of a spoon or a spatula. Return the tray to the freezer until completely set, about 30 minutes. To serve, remove from the freezer and cut into squares with a warm knife.

SERVES 8

Don't worry about washing the food processor between goes for this one. All the flavours are designed to be eaten together, and it won't affect the overall look.

A bit salty, a bit sweet,
a whole lotta sexy.

NO-BAKE CACAO and RASPBERRY CAKE with CREAMY CHOCOLATE ICING

Chocolate cakes should be rich, creamy and decadent, and that is exactly what this cake is. Even better, it's bake-free. Too easy!

Line a 22 cm springform cake tin with baking paper.

Place the dates and hazelnuts in a bowl, cover with boiling water and leave to soak for 30 minutes.

Once soaked, drain the dates and hazelnuts and place in a food processor with the cacao powder. Blitz until very smooth, then transfer to the prepared cake tin. Stir in the toasted pecans, cinnamon and the majority of the raspberries, reserving a few for decorating the top. Chill in the fridge for 2 hours.

Meanwhile, for the icing, blend all the ingredients in a food processor until smooth and creamy. Set aside in the fridge to keep firm.

Once chilled, take the cake out of the fridge and remove it from the tin. Coat all over with the icing and decorate with the remaining raspberries. You can sprinkle over some edible flower petals too, if you like. Enjoy this cake fresh from the fridge to keep the icing nice and firm!

SERVES 12

800 g medjool dates, pitted

400 g (3⅓ cups) hazelnuts

120 g (1 cup) cacao powder

100 g (1 cup) pecans, toasted and roughly chopped

2 tablespoons ground cinnamon

500 g (4 cups) fresh raspberries

edible flower petals (optional)

Creamy chocolate icing

4 ripe avocados

3 tablespoons maple syrup

2 tablespoons coconut cream, chilled until solid

200 g (1¾ cups) cacao powder

1 vanilla pod, split and scraped

'FERRERO ROCHER' TART

Who doesn't love Ferrero Rocher? They're decadent, luxurious and taste sensational. That's exactly why I wanted to bring those flavours to life in this incredible tart.

Base

200 g (2 cups) hazelnut meal

135 g (1½ cups) desiccated coconut

3 tablespoons maple syrup

150 g unsalted butter, melted

'Ferrero Rocher' filling

280 g (2 cups) blanched hazelnuts

185 ml (¾ cup) coconut cream

125 ml (½ cup) maple syrup

60 g (½ cup) cacao powder

1 vanilla pod, split and scraped

3 tablespoons coconut oil, melted

pinch of sea salt

To serve (optional)

Whipped Coconut Cream
(see page 213)

fresh berries

cacao nibs

toasted hazelnuts, crushed

Preheat the oven to 180°C and line a baking tray with baking paper. Grease a 22 cm loose-bottomed, circular, fluted flan tin with a little butter.

For the tart base, combine the hazelnut meal, desiccated coconut, maple syrup and melted butter in a bowl. Using your fingers, press the mixture firmly and evenly over the base and side of the prepared tin. Bake for 20 minutes, or until cooked and golden. Set aside.

For the filling, arrange the hazelnuts on the prepared baking tray in an even layer and toast for 10 minutes, or until lightly golden and fragrant. Transfer the nuts to a food processor along with the remaining filling ingredients and blend until well combined, smooth and creamy.

Spoon the filling mixture into the tart shell and spread evenly, then place in the fridge for at least 30 minutes to set. Enjoy as it is, or for something truly divine, serve it with your choice of whipped coconut cream, fresh berries or a sprinkling of cacao nibs or hazelnuts – or all of the above!

SERVES 8

RAW CHOC-BERRY CHEESECAKE

I have to admit I have quite the sweet tooth, and on my travels around Australia and the world I've stumbled across an amazing array of raw treats and desserts. One that I see pop up everywhere is raw cheesecake, and I couldn't put this book together without sharing this absolute favourite of mine.

90 g pitted medjool dates

200 g (2 cups) pecans

3 tablepoons desiccated coconut

60 g (½ cup) cacao powder

1 tablespoon maple syrup

1 tablespoon coconut oil, melted

1 teaspoon ground cinnamon

1 vanilla pod, split and scraped

cacao nibs, to serve

Berry cheese filling

320 g (2 cups) macadamia nuts, soaked for 2–4 hours or overnight, then drained and rinsed

250 ml (1 cup) Vanilla Almond Milk (see page 34)

125 ml (½ cup) coconut oil, melted

70 g coconut butter

1 vanilla pod, split and scraped

3 tablespoons maple syrup

250 g (2 cups) mixed berries, fresh or frozen and thawed

Line a 22 cm fluted tart or pie tin with baking paper.

Place the dates in a bowl, cover in boiling water and leave to soak for 10 minutes. Drain.

In the food processor, blitz together the pecans, desiccated coconut and cacao powder to form a fine crumb. Transfer it to a bowl and set aside.

Add the soaked dates, maple syrup, coconut oil, cinnamon and vanilla seeds to the food processor and pulse to form a thick, wet paste, then gradually stir in the pecan crumb mixture until well combined (you may need to turn it out onto your work surface and combine with your hands). Press the mixture into the prepared cake tin and transfer to the freezer for 10 minutes to firm up.

Meanwhile, make the filling. Blitz the soaked macadamia nuts in the food processor until thoroughly broken down. With the motor running, gradually add the remaining ingredients and continue to blend until creamy, smooth and free of lumps.

Remove the tin from the freezer, pour the filling over the base and spread evenly. Return to the freezer for 2 hours to chill and set.

Remove the cheesecake from the freezer and let it sit at room temperature for 20–30 minutes before serving. Scatter over some cacao nibs and cut it into slices with a hot knife.

SERVES 10

RAW 'SNICKERS' CAKE

This is a no-bake cake that will leave you wanting more. There are a few different processes involved but it's worth it, and once you've finished you will be so impressed with what you have created. I can't promise it will last long, but hey, food was designed to be enjoyed!

Grease and line a 22 cm springform cake tin with baking paper.

To make the base, put all the ingredients in a food processor and pulse together until the mixture resembles fine breadcrumbs. Press the mixture into the base of the prepared tin in an even layer, being sure to get it right into the edge all the way around, then chill in the freezer for 10–15 minutes.

For the filling, place the macadamia nuts, almond milk, coconut oil, dates, vanilla seeds and salt in the food processor and pulse to a smooth paste.

Remove the tin from the freezer and pour half the filling mixture over the base. Sprinkle over the toasted hazelnuts and return to the freezer to set for a further 20 minutes.

Add the cacao powder to the remaining filling mixture and pulse again until well combined. Remove the tin from the freezer, pour the mixture over the first filling layer, then return to the freezer to set.

For the topping, place the coconut oil, cacao powder, hazelnut butter, maple syrup, vanilla seeds and salt in the food processor and pulse together for 3–5 minutes, or until everything is smooth and creamy.

Remove the cake from the tin and drizzle the chocolate topping in a zig zag pattern over the top. Scatter over the toasted hazelnuts and some cacao nibs to finish, then chill in the fridge until the topping is set. To serve, leave the cake at room temperature for 5 minutes before cutting with a warm knife.

SERVES 10

Base

155 g (1 cup) cashew nuts

60 g (1 cup) shredded coconut

2 tablespoons cacao powder

1 tablespoon maple syrup

3 tablespoons coconut oil, melted

1 vanilla pod, split and scraped

pinch of sea salt

'Snickers' filling

240 g (1½ cups) macadamia nuts, soaked for 2–4 hours or overnight, then drained and rinsed

250 ml (1 cup) Vanilla Almond Milk (see page 34)

125 ml (½ cup) coconut oil, melted

12 medjool dates, pitted

1 vanilla pod, split and scraped

pinch of sea salt

70 g (½ cup) hazelnuts, toasted and crushed

50 g (½ cup) cacao powder

Topping

125 ml (½ cup) coconut oil, melted

3 tablespoons cacao powder

75 g hazelnut butter

1 tablespoon maple syrup

1 vanilla pod, split and scraped

pinch of sea salt

70 g (½ cup) hazelnuts, toasted and crushed

cacao nibs, to serve

THANK YOU!

This book is an absolute dream come true. I'm incredibly blessed to have been given the opportunity to share with the world my immense passion for living our best lives through healthy food. The road to this exciting release has been shared with a number of very important players who I credit with making it possible to be in a position to write this today. To you all, I am extremely grateful; as I know I wouldn't be the man I am today without your love, support and belief in me.

Mary Small, from day one you have guided me with such incredible trust, belief and professionalism to evolve as an author. The author I was when I met you is worlds away from the one standing here today, having learnt from your expertise, passion and incredible knowledge. Words cannot describe how thankful I am for your belief in me. Your laugh is infectious and it can turn a good day into a great one. So much love your way.

Clare Marshall, you have taken my pages of words and turned them into an epic book, and given me such a sense of safety and security knowing it was in your hands. Your energy is so calming and your eye for detail is inspiring. Thanks for always smiling and being so easy to work with. You're a dream to have as part of this book.

Jane Winning, thanks for guiding me through the creation, development and delivery of what I see as an incredible team effort. I can certainly come up with my favourite recipes, but it is your hard work and commitment that gave it structure and soul. Such a pleasure to have worked with you.

Kirby Armstrong, thank you for creating the most beautiful look and feel for this baby of mine whilst you were having a baby of your own. You have given each and every page such love and warmth and it truly brings the food and words to life.

Lee Blaylock, on the day I walked into that house and saw the props for styling, I thought I had died and gone to heaven! Your eye for detail, finesse in finishing and overall clear vision of what this book would look like is what makes you world class. I am so grateful.

Mark Roper, I had heard your name through the years and couldn't believe I was lucky enough to get to work with you. The magic you created under our dark curtain cave can never be spoken about. First rule of the black room: never talk about what happens in the black room. You're such a legend, thanks!

Emma Warren, I think you officially turned me from a home cook into your apprentice on this shoot! My lord, is there anything you don't know how to cook?

You took my recipes and helped me polish them to perfection. Not only are you a dream to work with, but I can now read your handwriting!

Emma Christian, every time you rocked in the door in the morning I could tell because the place felt happier and brighter. Thanks for the chats and the laughs and, of course, for helping make this dream a reality.

Kylie McAllester, I will be sending your copy of this book to Japan, you legend! Thanks so much for your handy work behind the scenes, and I hope all your worldly dreams are coming true.

Simon Davis, thanks for coping with my spelling, grammar and overall creation of new words that don't exist yet! You have added such clarity to my words and thoughts, and for that I am grateful.

Deb Kaloper, although we only worked together for one day, being able to connect with you was so awesome. I love your energy and you are such a calming soul to have on a shoot.

Nelly le Comte, you are the definition of loving what you do. There were no limits to getting the shots you envisioned. From waiting for the perfect sunlight to going on our Casuarina adventure, thank you for being a delight to work with.

Ty, my better half, my brains and my beauty. You have put up with recipes that don't work, grocery bills that exceed normality and kitchen messes like no others. You are incredibly patient when I am writing, forgiving when I am stressed, calming when I have a deadline and loving no matter what. Together we are fathers to our baby dragon and the creators of our massive future.

Mum and Dad, you deserve all the credit in the world for standing by me through thick and thin. I love you both very much.

Pete Evans, mate, wow! Who would have thought you'd go from eliminating me on *My Kitchen Rules* to becoming one of my mates and colleagues? Your advice, guidance, belief and hard work has shaped me into a better man.

Scott Gooding, we have come massively far, mate, and I am so proud of us both. I am excited to see our next professional endeavours take off, and I wouldn't be here today without our incredible runs on the board.

To all of my supporters, believers and followers. Without your love for my recipes, commitment to living a fantastic life and loyalty in supporting what I do, none of this would be possible. I hope to be able to give back in some way to each and every one of you.

INDEX

A Plum book
First published in 2016 by
Pan Macmillan Australia Pty Limited
Level 25, 1 Market Street,
Sydney, NSW 2000, Australia

Level 1, 15–19 Claremont Street,
South Yarra, Victoria 3141, Australia

Text copyright © Luke Hines 2016
Photographs copyright © Mark Roper 2016, except photos of the author on
pages 1, 8–9, 16, 38, 60–1, 75, 94–5, 103, 123, 148–9, 154, 202–3, 222 and
246–7 © Nelly le Comte

The moral right of the author has been asserted.

Design by Kirby Armstrong
Edited by Simon Davis
Index by Hannah Koelmeyer, Tusk Studio
Photography by Mark Roper (with additional photography by Nelly le Comte)
Prop and food styling by Lee Blaylock
Front cover prop and food styling by Deborah Kaloper
Food preparation by Emma Christian, Kylie McAllester and Emma Warren
Typeset by Pauline Haas
Colour reproduction by Splitting Image Colour Studio
Printed and bound in China by Imago Printing International Limited

A CIP catalogue record for this book is available from the
National Library of Australia.

All rights reserved. No part of this book may be reproduced or transmitted by any
person or entity (including Google, Amazon or similar organisations), in any form or
means, electronic or mechanical, including photocopying, recording, scanning or by
any information storage and retrieval system, without prior permission in writing from
the publisher. The publishers and their respective employees, agents and authors are
not liable for injuries or damage occasioned to any person as a result of reading or
following the information contained in this book. It is recommended that individually
tailored advice is sought from your healthcare or medical professional. We advise that
the information contained in this book does not negate personal responsibility on the
part of the reader for their own health and safety.

The publisher would like to thank the following for their generosity in providing props
for the book: AURA by Tracie Ellis and Shiko Pottery.

10 9 8 7 6 5 4 3